Willington in the First World War

Robert Bollington

Best wishes

Rob Bollington

First published in 2018 by the Gostwick Press, Willington

for Willington Local History Group

Sources of illustrations

Figures 1 and 18 and the front cover photographs of two men named on the Willington Rolls of Honour - Jack Webb (left; 1st Battalion, Bedfordshire Regiment) and Fred Cooper (right; 6th Battalion, Bedfordshire Regiment) are from the Willington Local History Group archives. Figure 22 (Z153/46) is included courtesy of the Bedfordshire Archives Service. Figures 3, 4, 9, 12, 13, 15, 16, 17 and 20 are from photographs of items in the Bedfordshire Times and Independent. Figure 7 is from the records of St Lawrence Church, Willington. Figures 2, 8 and 11 and the extract from the diary of Madeline Whitbread are included courtesy of the Southill Chattels. Figure 10 and the quotations from Joyce Godber are included courtesy of Richard and Candy Godber. Figures 21, 23, 24, 25, 26 and appendix 1 are photographs taken by the author and figure 19 is from a wartime postcard in the author's possession. The frontispiece, the extract from the memories of Reginald Lymon, and the photograph on the back cover of his grandfather are courtesy of Douglas Craft.

Frontispiece: Postcard showing Harry Spavins (front row, 3rd from left) during training at Haynes Park

Contents

Introduction iii

The Eve of War 1

War and Mobilisation 5

The Church and Vicar 15

Support for the Troops 18

Soldiers in the Area 24

Emergency Planning and Wartime Controls 27

Village Life and Work...35

Soldiers at the Front 47

After the War 70

Appendix 1 – The Willington Roll of Honour in the church....78

Appendix 2 – Serving men with a Willington connection 79

Endnotes 93

Introduction

This is the story of the Bedfordshire village of Willington during the First World War. The account is written on the centenary of the War's end and my hope is that it will encourage others to share stories in their own families. I have relied on newspaper reports, military records, census returns, electoral registers, diaries, individual memories and letters. Some of this material is from the archives of the Bedfordshire Archives Service, Willington Local History Group and the Southill Estate. I would especially like to acknowledge help from Douglas Craft, whose family fought in the War and who generously shared his own research. I am also grateful to Sue Harland, Nigel Lutt and Gordon Vowles for their thoughtful feedback.

While my focus is on the experience of one village, with its farms, nurseries and market gardens, I have tried to provide a wider context. The Roll of Honour in the village church lists sixty-eight men who served and the war memorial names sixteen who died. Most were in the army and involved on the Western Front or around the Mediterranean. Those left at home worked hard to provide 'comforts' for the troops while facing a raft of wartime regulations and restrictions. Maintaining food supplies against the backdrop of the wartime labour shortage was vital to victory and a pressing local issue.

Key figures in the village took a prominent role on the Home Front. Isaac Godber, the village's leading nurseryman, encouraged recruitment and acted as a special constable, with responsibility for dealing with the threat of air raids and invasion. His wife, Bessie, while managing a large family, registered women for employment and took care of the soldiers billeted in their house. The school's headmistress, Miss Elizabeth Buckingham, encouraged the children's efforts to provide material 'comforts' for the troops. The Vicar, Rev Frederick Kingston, provided spiritual comfort, conducting services in memory of the fallen. All were relative newcomers in a village that had changed and grown in the decade immediately before the War.

While fatalities in Willington were proportionately high, the village's experiences do resonate with the more general experience of what was then called the Great War. This is above all a story of how everyday life was transformed and is one that should not be forgotten. As I tell the story, I should add that the interpretations are my own and do not necessarily represent the views of others in Willington Local History Group.

Robert Bollington, 2018

The Eve of War

The contrast between the summer of 1914[1] and the horrors of war has often been made. On the eve of war, people enjoyed the usual summer activities. However, tensions in Ireland, suffragette militancy, industrial unrest and rivalry between nations created the sense that the world was changing.

This picture was mirrored in Willington. In late July 1914, a garden party and sale of work was held at the vicarage to raise funds for a village hall. Reports described this as 'an ideal village holiday' and the garden as 'gay with splashes of colour' with various stalls, a tent for teas and a platform decorated with flowers and flags. There were games such as billiards, hoop-la, croquet, clock golf and 'bumble puppy'. Village children performed, and a comedy sketch was presented by adults. A string band played on into the evening. 'Great fun' was had when 'a couple of fowls were liberated in a field for the married women to catch and catching was keeping. The chase was long and exciting, but ultimately the poultry came off second best.'[2]

This cosy scene was far removed from what was to come. It also reflected how the village had changed. For as long as anyone could remember, Willington had been a farming community and part of the estates of the Duke of Bedford. That ended in 1902, when

Herbrand, the eleventh Duke of Bedford, sold Willington and Cople to two speculators, George and Arthur James Keeble of Peterborough. The Duke wanted to diversify his income and invest money from the sale in shares and bonds. The agricultural depression at the end of the nineteenth century had led to people leaving villages such as Willington. It had also meant the costs of taxation and estate management were greater than the falling income from rents. Faced with possible land reform and death duties, landowners felt on the defensive. While Herbrand was a pioneer in the sale of landed estates, many other landowners in Bedfordshire and elsewhere took the same approach.

The purchasers of Willington and Cople, the Keeble brothers, divided the villages into lots and sold these at six auctions between 1902 and 1907. To help the sales, the Keeble brothers campaigned for a railway station to add to the siding in Willington and this duly opened in 1903. The advertisements for the auctions referred to 'highly desirable freehold agricultural and market gardening and sporting estates' and to the benefits of the railway.

The plan to attract market gardeners to Willington was successful. While some of the lots were bought by existing inhabitants, newcomers came in and transformed the village. The new arrivals included people who came to play a key role in village life. Among them were Isaac Godber, who began moving his nursery business to Willington from Kempston, and Mark Young (the elder) of Sandy, a farmer, market gardener, seed grower and gravel merchant.

The auctions and the opening of the railway station in 1903 stimulated the growth of Willington. The 1911 census reveals the extent of the transformation. The population had risen to 370 from 204 at the time of the 1901 census, when it was in decline. While there were still many jobs on farms or in service, there were now also nurserymen and market gardeners and their labourers. They were joined by a station master, railway porter, publican, estate agent, surveyor, insurance agent and artist. New houses now complemented the older thatched dwellings and model estate cottages. All in all, Willington had changed significantly from the days when it formed part of the Bedford estates.

Rev Augustus Orlebar, Vicar of Willington for fifty-four years, died in 1912, an event that symbolised the end of an era. It was his successor, Rev Frederick Kingston, who hosted the fete and faced the challenge of providing pastoral and spiritual support during the War. Other newcomers joined him and villagers of longer standing at the fete and together faced the War to come.

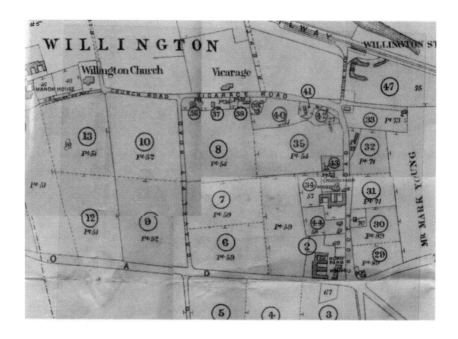

Figure 1: extract from sale catalogue showing some of the lots

The War was to have a profound effect on both those who went off to serve and those who remained at home. Supplying and feeding soldiers and civilians, paying the huge costs, and dealing with attacks at home and abroad necessitated an unprecedented level of state control. When the War started many were optimistic that it would be over quickly. Instead it became a long, complex struggle on a massive scale, with technology, resources and morale key to the eventual outcome. Everyone had a part to play. We will now look at what this meant locally.

War and Mobilisation

The assassination of the Austrian Archduke, Franz Ferdinand and his wife, Sophie, by a Bosnian terrorist on June 28th, 1914 was the catalyst for War. Austria-Hungary, with German backing, blamed Serbia and took steps to crush it. This set off a chain reaction that brought the major powers to war. Britain, committed to preserving Belgian neutrality and unwilling to stand aside as Germany threatened to dominate Europe, went to war on August 4th, 1914. At the outset, the Entente powers, Britain, France and Russia fought against the Central Powers, Germany and Austria-Hungary. As the War progressed, other powers entered and fighting spread across the world.

We get a local reaction to the start of the War from Madeline Whitbread of nearby Southill. She was to play a key role on the Home Front in Bedfordshire and was the wife of Samuel Howard Whitbread, the County's Lord Lieutenant and Education Committee chairman. She reacted to news of War in her diary entry for August 5th, 1914:

> *"We are at war. Like an awful nightmare appears all life to one. It's as if one was sleep walking – It's come on one so suddenly as to be incredible."*

She was very aware of the costs of war and what was at stake as her entries for August 18th and September 1st, 1914 show:

> *"It makes one shiver when one thinks of the carnage which must take place when at last all the millions of men meet in the horror of a battle."*

Figure 2: Madeline Whitbread

"Our whole existence is at stake. If we don't win, then good bye to the British Empire and all it stands for – the Germans have

burnt Louvain and all its treasures. Its museums, its cathedral – gone – that such uncivilized barbarities can be contemplated, much less carried out, makes one dizzy with amazement but the cruelties they practice towards the inhabitants make one see red."

Figure 3: recruitment advertisement

As hostilities became imminent reservists were called up. Then came the drive to recruit volunteers led by Lord Kitchener, the newly appointed Secretary of State for War. Both locally and nationally, newspapers, posters and speakers all urged men to do their bit. Prominent people took a lead with stirring patriotic speeches at recruiting meetings.

There are reports of Isaac Godber, the village's leading nurseryman, chairing and addressing a recruiting meeting in nearby Cople in October 1914[3]. Samuel Howard Whitbread and Madeline went around the villages in the area urging men to enlist as the following entry from Madeline's diary shows:

> *"Howard has been told to recruit & so he & I have gone to 2 or 3 meetings for every night for a fortnight. We roll out in the car through the peaceful, lovely land till we come to some little village, where a crowd is awaiting us and there, standing on a cart or in one case on the stone steps of the old stone cross in the market place, Howard delivers his oration. And Black, the Liberal member & Prothero, the Unionist member proffered [to] stand with us & speak. For all politics & parties are overlaid with 'All for England leit motif'.*

> *I watch in the gathering darkness the sturdy yokels' faces. Poor lads - they dimly realize that somewhere there is such a storm raging that perchance, it may sweep them from their safe moorings into the great sea beyond. A few always come up after every meeting & more the next day when relieved from the gaping stair [sic] of the village folk, they give in their names*

and declare themselves ready to go and do their bit. At one meeting there was a young man who was just going to put up his hand to signify his intention to do joining, when elbowing her way madly through the crowd, her face alive with anguish and passion, a stalwart girl, his 3 months wife, flung her arms about him & absolutely dragged him away.

Poor souls! Poor souls! How should they understand that those boys will be the men who will prevent those cruel Huns from treating us in England as the miserable people of Louvain and Termonde were treated.

And then after the meeting is over while Howard takes the names of the recruits, I distribute among the crowd a little leaflet I had compiled setting out the allowances the Government allow and saying why we want them to join, and then home the cool night air blowing in our faces & the cheers of the people ringing in our ears."

Something of the atmosphere and social dynamics of the 1914 recruitment meetings is also captured in the following report about a recruitment meeting in Gamlingay that appeared in the *Bedfordshire Times and Independent* on September 4th, 1914:

"A meeting was called Friday evening, August 28th, in the Council School, of all men between the ages of 19 and 30. Mr. J. Fowler took the chair and delivered a very earnest address on the needs of the country for more soldiers. They were fighting for their freedom, for their own existence as a nation, and for the continued freedom of the independent States. All who were able should join Lord Kitchener's Army at once. Captain E. St Quintin, who fought during the Boer War at Ladysmith, described the terms and conditions of service. Mr. A. S. Orlebar

*followed and made an earnest appeal to the young men present
to join the Army. This was accentuated by Mrs. M. Wentworth
Stanley, who represented the Soldiers' and Sailors' Association.
The meeting was crowded, and enthusiastic and patriotic songs
were sung at intervals. At the close ten names were given the
Committee, and the following day 11 additional names were
received. The following Monday, the recruits assembled at the
Cross, and received an enthusiastic send-off from the large
crowd. They were taken to the recruiting headquarters at
Cambridge in motor cars provided by Mr. Briscoe, Mr. Pym, Mr.
Newton, Colonel Duncombe, Lord Clifden and Mr. A. S. Orlebar,
while cars in reserve were provided by Mr. Lomax and Major
Stanley. All were accepted at Cambridge, and on Wednesday
morning the recruits went to the centre for training. The
recruits were warmly complimented at Cambridge for the public
and patriotic spirit they had shown."*

Possibly one of those joining up was Herbert Ray, who grew up in
Gamlingay and whose family later moved to Willington.

Figure 4: men queueing to enlist in Bedford

By the end of 1914, according to a correspondent of the Bedford newspaper[4], 'concerned for the honour of Willington', fourteen men from Willington had responded and were in the armed forces while five had been refused. Several others had signed to say they were willing to serve if called upon to do so. The publicity, anger at reported German atrocities in Belgium, recruitment meetings such as those described above and social pressure all had had their effect.

By March 1915, the number from Willington serving had risen to twenty-seven, according to a survey carried out by elementary school head teachers and published in the Bedford newspaper. This represented 7.29% of the 1911 population and was above the average of 5.48% for the villages in the survey and roughly the same as for Cople. The highest level of recruitment in Bedfordshire villages at that time was in Cardington, which stood at 11.8%[5].

As the War progressed, it became clear that relying on volunteers was not enough and in January 1916 the Military Service Act introduced conscription for single men, initially aged 18 to 41. In May 1916, a second act extended conscription to married men in the same age range, a range also later extended. Exemptions were possible for those doing work of national importance, the sole supporters of dependents, the medically unfit, and approved conscientious objectors.

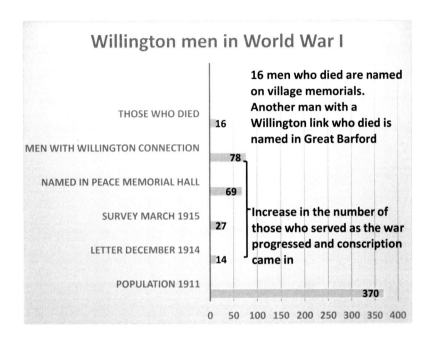

Figure 5: Willington men serving in World War I

Conscription led to an increase in the number of Willington men involved. There were also cases where men sought exemption from being called up, typically on the grounds they were doing full-time work of national importance on the land. These cases were heard at the Bedford Rural Tribunal and, if disputed, at the Bedfordshire Appeals' Tribunal.

In January 1920, a return by the Willington Parish Council named sixty-two men who had taken part in the War, noting the list was as 'correct as possible.'[6] According to the Roll of Honour in St Lawrence church, sixty-eight men served[7]. One further name, that of Claude R. Davison, appears on the Roll of Honour in the Peace Memorial Hall. The 1918 Absent Voters' Register, the Parish Council minutes, and military records suggest there may have been others with some connection to the village, giving a potential total of seventy-eight. Complete accuracy was and remains difficult to achieve, given the scale of the conflict and changes in rank, regiment and residence.

Given the discrepancies in the surviving records and their incompleteness, it is only possible to arrive at an approximate breakdown of the men who served by rank and regiment. Bearing this caution in mind, some thirty per cent of the Willington men who served are known to have done so with the Bedfordshire Regiment at some stage. Only one man, Claude R. Davison, was an officer. He came from Sandy originally and appears on the 1918 Willington Absent Voters' Register as a 2nd Lieutenant. Of the other men with at least some connection with the village, forty-five were privates, ten were drivers, five were gunners, three were sappers, five were corporals, lance corporals or acting corporals and four were sergeants, (including a lance sergeant and a Company Quartermaster Sergeant or CQMS). There was also a guardsman, a rifleman and an aircraftman 2nd class (AC2). The ranks of two are not known.

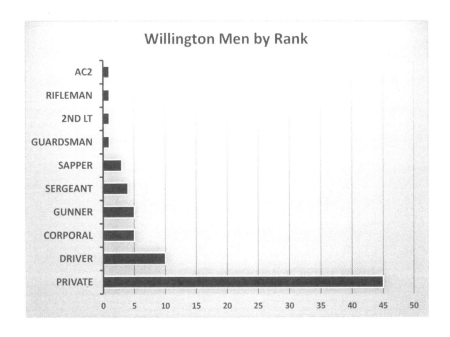

Figure 6: Willington men by rank

Most Willington men who served were manual workers before the War, mostly working on farms, market gardens and nurseries, or were the sons of manual workers and still at school at the time of the 1911 census. Three men, George Franklin, Thomas Henry Golder and Frank Farr, were serving soldiers and a few others had served in the Bedfordshire militia for a time. The future wartime officer, Claude R. Davison, was at school in Margate and after the War became a farmer like his father and brothers.

The men, not engaged in manual work before the War, included Willington's own 'man from the Pru,' Albert Hales, who originally came from Sheffield, and Cannon Cross and William Golder, who were milk salesmen.

The impact of War was felt keenly in the village. Efforts were made to collect money and to provide 'comforts' to help the troops. Soldiers on their way to war joined in village events and were billeted in the village. Plans were made for possible invasion or attack. We turn to these features of the Home Front next before moving on to the men who fought.

The Church and Vicar

In 1913, Rev Frederick Kingston became Vicar of Willington. Like his predecessor, the long serving Rev Augustus Orlebar, Kingston was a keen sportsman and had strong academic tastes. He led the church during the War and afterwards until his death in 1933. He was supported by his unmarried sister, Mary Kingston, who lived with him at the Vicarage.

On the eve of War, on August 2nd, 1914, Kingston preached on the themes of 'the raging of the nations' and 'England's duty in the crisis.' Later in the year, on November 8th, he preached on the theme of 'laying down life for friends' and a week later his theme was 'self-sacrifice.' In the same month, he gave a pulpit tribute to Field Marshal Lord Roberts of Boer War fame, who had recently died, with the organist playing the Dead March at the close of the service. This all mirrored the patriotic and optimistic mood of 1914.

Figure 7: Rev Frederick Kingston

As the impact of war became clear and hope of a quick victory vanished, Kingston reflected a more sombre mood. He wrote a poem, 'A Tribute to Our Boys,' that appeared in the Bedford newspaper in November 1915, where he spoke of 'maidens heart-oppressed' mourning the 'loss of their beloved boys,' boys who 'the call of duty one by one obeyed and perished – on the verge of manhood's dawn.' The poem goes on:

> *"For every canon shot, a grave, a cross!*
> *For every cross, sad hearts at home that ache!*
> *Oh pray, if haply gain may come from loss,*
> *And midnight gloom in morning glory break!"*

The church service register lists memorial services held during the War for some of those who died: George Franklin (June 27th, 1915), William and Arthur Golder (May 13th, 1917), Daniel Gudgin (April 28th, 1918), Edgar Swannell (June 16th, 1918) and Herbert Ray (July 21st, 1918). At the memorial service for Daniel Gudgin, Kingston spoke on the theme of 'hath God forgotten' and at the service for Herbert Ray, his theme was 'are war sufferings to be in vain.'

The Vicar's second poem published in the Bedford newspaper appeared in May 1918. This was entitled 'Over the Top.' This poem paints a graphic picture of trench warfare:

> *"Over the top they are gone the brave boys*
> *Over the top they are gone*
> *Out of the shelter of friendly caves*
> *Into the welter of flaming waves*
> *Into the medley of frenzy and noise*
> *Pelted by shells as they plash through mire*
> *Torn by the fangs of the serpent wire*
> *Over the top at the word of command*

Over the top into No Man's Land
Over the top they are gone."

The poem ends with a consolatory statement of belief that 'over the top the true hearted and brave are speeding to paradise land.' The Vicar's words reflect the sacrifices that were made and the human costs of the War. As he became aware of these, he appears to have maintained his faith in better things to come.

Support for the Troops

One of the main concerns in the village during the War was to provide 'comforts' for the troops in the form of socks, scarves, shirts, tobacco and other items that would make life a little more comfortable and serve as a reminder of home. Money was also raised to support a range of wartime needs and emergencies.

What was done in Willington often contributed to a County or national campaign. Prominent people such as Madeline Whitbread and public bodies such as the Bedfordshire Education Committee encouraged efforts across the County. A report in the Bedford newspaper, on October 23rd, 1914, referred to a Willington whist drive and dance. This raised money to buy material to make garments for the troops. On November 25th, 1914, the village headmistress, Miss Buckingham, noted in the school log book that one dozen pairs of socks had been sent to Madeline Whitbread for the soldiers. A Bedford newspaper report on December 4th, 1914 mentioned a social that paid for material for seventeen flannel shirts for the soldiers at the Front, made by a working party at the Vicarage that met on Thursday afternoons. On December 25th, 1914, a similar report noted that a Willington 'work at home' party led by Florence Cope had forwarded twenty-four pairs of socks to Madeline Whitbread. In addition, the village children led by Emily Kitton had made fifty-one garments for the Belgian refugee children.

This type of effort continued throughout the War. For example, on November 3rd, 1915, Miss Buckingham noted that the school had despatched 23 garments for soldiers and sailors to Shire Hall, Bedford. On January 14th, 1916, the Bedford newspaper quoted a letter thanking one of the Willington school children for the warm garments they had sent. He wrote:

> *"I received your welcome gift the same night that I was going into the trenches, and I am writing from the front line with the muffler wrapped around my ears. I am in my dug-out just 150 yards from the Germans, and as all our large guns are firing the noise is awful. If you could see me now, plastered with mud from head to foot, you would think me a very comical soldier – not at all like the smart soldiers in and around Bedford."*

Just after the War ended, but well before the end of demobilisation, Miss Buckingham noted that on November 18th, 1918 one dozen pairs of socks for the troops had been dispatched to Shire Hall.

As well as items of clothing, tobacco was sent to the troops. For example, in August 1915 it was reported that Muriel Mayes had raised money to buy tobacco for the soldiers. She subsequently received some thank-you post cards from soldiers:

> *"We are just out of the trenches after 28 days. I hope your kindness will be rewarded with an everlasting peace."*

> *"We are very grateful for the cigarettes; they came just right. It is a marvel what a smoke will do; it helps to pass away many an hour of watching and waiting in the trenches."*

Over the course of the War, the aim of social evenings and other fund-raising initiatives was sometimes to help a specific cause, such as the Belgian or French Relief Funds, the Red Cross or the British Prisoners of War Fund. The church sent money in 1914 for the Belgian Relief Fund. On April 23rd, 1915, the Bedford newspaper reported a penny collection in the village for the Red Cross. On July 23rd, 1915, it was reported that the school children had collected money for Dr Barnardo's Homes and the French Relief Fund. On March 28th, 1918, Miss Buckingham noted a collection made by the scholars for the British Prisoners of War Fund amounting to £3/10/-.

Figure 8: Madeline Whitbread in front of a fund-raising stall

By 1915, the idea of raising money for a Soldiers' Christmas Gifts Fund to send Christmas gifts to Willington servicemen had been established under the leadership of the Vicar. Gifts of a vest, soap, nightlights, a pipe, tobacco, cigarettes and sweets were sent to those in the trenches. Transport drivers were sent motor gloves rather than vests. Those serving at home received gloves, a pipe, tobacco and sweets. The friends of the killed and missing were also to receive an appropriate gift as a memorial. This practice continued with comparable gifts sent in each subsequent year.

The Government had to finance the huge costs of the War and to do so extended and increased income tax, encouraged citizens to lend it money via the War Loan, and borrowed heavily from the USA. In 1915, some of the school children bought vouchers to exchange for £5 of the War Loan. In the same spirit, the committee set up to procure a Parish Room, agreed to use £20 of their funds to buy land for a building and to put the balance of £30 into the War Loan.

Support also involved care for wounded soldiers and a concern for the health and welfare of the troops. During the War, the Joint War Committee of the British Red Cross and the Order of St John worked to provide a range of services, such as organising volunteers as nurses and creating working parties to make clothing and other items for hospitals. One working party was run from 48 Harpur Street in Bedford by Eleanor Paine[8], who was well known in the area for developing district nursing and for her work in first aid. This working party made over 42,000 slippers for hospitals at home and abroad. Materials, such as carpet, were purchased from collections at annual Bedford slipper days and donated from the USA and elsewhere. Mrs Paine's group involved four Willington women, Amy Balmer of St Albans Cottage, Florence Cope of Stone Croft, Fanny Davison of Scarsdale, and Harriet Preston of Sunnyside. The four women put in a combined total of about 3500 hours, making slippers for wounded soldiers.

Figure 9: Nurses at the Ampthill Road Schools Voluntary Aid Detachment (VAD) Hospital, Bedford

Another woman, Annie Woodhead, who had recently moved to Brandesburton in Willington, volunteered as a nurse at the Ampthill Road Schools Voluntary Aid Detachment (VAD) Hospital, Bedford. This began as a hospital for Highland soldiers stricken with measles and later treated the wounded.

The health of the troops was also supported in other ways. For example, in September 1917, Miss Buckingham reported that her pupils spent several days picking blackberries for the soldiers and sailors. This was to support a nationwide jam making campaign. The

Bedford newspaper of September 7th, 1917 referred to the campaign as designed:

> "to facilitate the collection of blackberries by school children for the manufacture of jam for the Navy and Army. This has been done at the request of the Food Production Dept., acting on behalf of the Admiralty and the War Office. It is of great importance that a very large quantity of blackberries, which have a special medicinal value and are important for the health of the troops, should be collected."

By the end of the campaign, the County's school children had collected an impressive 30 tons of fruit with pride of place going to Wootton, where 3½ cwt was collected.

The various types of support given provided an important link between the Home Front and the soldiers. The efforts also reflected how the War permeated all aspects of life. What happened in Willington was typical in both County and country.

Soldiers in the Area

Highland regiments and other soldiers passed through the Bedford area on their way to the Front and Willington experienced this at first hand. For example, on September 9th, 1914, the village headmistress, Miss Buckingham, noted that one of her staff, Miss Winchester, was unable to return as the railway was closed to the public for the conveyance of troops. Later in the year, on December 18th, 1914, the Bedford paper reported a route march by the Scottish Battalions through Ravensden, Wilden, Great Barford, Willington and Fenlake.

Figure 10: Isaac and Bessie Godber

On March 15th, 1915, the Vicar made a note in the service register of the arrival of the Westmorland and Cumberland Yeomanry in the village, where they were billeted, and on June 28th, 1915, Miss Buckingham noted that three children billeted with the soldiers had left the village. Joyce Godber, the daughter of Isaac and Bessie Godber, remembered some of these soldiers being billeted at the Manor:

> *"Soon came the billeting of soldiers; 8 men of the Westmorland and Cumberland Yeomanry were billeted in the house and had*

to be cooked for in addition to the household of ten, besides occupying the morning room and two bedrooms. The men were country bred and good fellows. One once came back drunk but Bessie[9] spoke her mind and it never happened again. The maid at the time, Elsie Swannell was not of the most energetic. She was liable to small ailments and it was noticeable that she recovered when the soldiers were back in the evening. After Bessie had once refused to let her go up when evening came, there was an improvement."

A newspaper report on July 23rd, 1915 refers to a village whist drive and social, at which the prize winners were 1st Gunner Wells and 2nd Private Buckle. There was singing from the choir of the 4th Monmouths conducted by Corporal Jones and one of those present also sang 'Bonny banks of Loch Lomond.' Later that year (December 3rd, 1915), there was a report of another social, at which Welsh soldiers were also present and which ended with them singing the Welsh National Anthem in Welsh. The 4th Monmouths also attended a village whist drive and social evening, reported in the Bedford newspaper on February 4th, 1916, designed to raise money for the Red Cross. The report mentioned they were billeted nearby in Cople and Cardington.

The other soldiers in the area were those who came home on leave or after being discharged because they had been wounded or released to work on the land. Miss Buckingham noted in the school log book on February 1st, 1918 that Miss Moor, the infant teacher, had been given leave of absence that afternoon to spend time with a relative home from the Front. Among the Willington men discharged after being wounded who returned home before the War ended was Charles Wooding. He had enlisted in September 1914 and served in France with the 2nd Battalion, Bedfordshire Regiment. He was wounded at the battle of Loos in September 1915 and moved to hospital in Lincoln before being discharged in September 1916.

Emergency Planning and Wartime Controls

The impact of the War on day to day life was quickly apparent as reservists were called up, volunteers were recruited, and soldiers were stationed in the area. Advice appeared in newspapers during the first week of the War on suitable conduct in the circumstances:

> *"First and foremost. Keep your heads. Be calm. And go about your ordinary business quietly and soberly. Do not indulge in excitement or foolish demonstrations. Secondly. Think of others more than you are wont to do. Think of your duty to your neighbour. Think of the common weal. Try to contribute your share doing your duty in your own place and your own sphere. Be abstemious and economical. Avoid waste. Do not store goods and create an artificial scarcity to the hurt of others. Remember that it is an act of mean and selfish cowardice. Do not hoard gold. Let it circulate.*
>
> *Try make things easier, not more difficult. Remember those who are worse off than yourself. Pay punctually what you owe,*

especially to your poorest creditors, such as washerwomen and charwomen. If you are an employer think of your employed. Give them work and wages as long as you can and work short time rather than close down. If you are employed remember the difficulties of your employer. Instead of dwelling on your own privations think of the infinitely worse state of those who live at the seat of war and are not only thrown out of work but deprived of all they possess.

Do what you can to cheer and encourage our soldiers. Gladly help any organisation for their comfort and welfare. Explain to the young and the ignorant what war is, and why we have been forced to wage it.

To this we add: Let everyone who can, grow Autumn vegetables in his garden. Any seedsman will advise what to sow."[10]

Suitable behaviour was, however, not just encouraged by exhortations and advice of this nature. During the War, people were subject to new and progressively far reaching levels of control. This was done under the provisions of the Defence of the Realm Act (DORA), rushed into law in August 1914 and amended and extended six times during the conflict. Regulations under this legislation eventually covered most aspects of life. DORA and its amendments gave the Government wide-ranging powers, such as the authority to requisition factories and land needed for the war effort. Houses could be requisitioned for billeting soldiers. A variety of offences were created including helping the enemy by talking about naval or military matters in public places and spreading rumours or false or damaging reports about military affairs. Press censorship and censorship of communications from the Front were imposed. A variety of measures took effect to counter the threat of air raids, such as bans on bonfires and flying kites and ringing church bells, when lighting restrictions were in force.

In a bid to increase productivity, the legislation was used to restrict pub opening hours, regulate the strength of alcoholic drinks and ban treating or buying drinks for others. British Summer Time was introduced, again with boosting productivity in mind.

Figure 11: Samuel Howard Whitbread, Lord Lieutenant of Bedfordshire

Emergency planning measures were put in place to deal with the threat of enemy invasion or attack. Imposed across the country, these regulations and measures aimed to place the country's resources at the disposal of the war effort. Military needs came first. The measures affected Bedfordshire including Willington, just as they did all other parts of the country.

On October 16th, 1914, the Home Office wrote to Samuel Howard Whitbread as Lord Lieutenant of Bedfordshire requiring him to put in place measures to prepare for possible invasion. This was to be done through a Central Committee for the County overseeing Local Emergency Committees for each district. The committees had to make plans to prevent the enemy getting hold of transport, livestock and food stuff. They had to work out ways of destroying bridges, railways and the like on receipt of military orders and of keeping roads clear for military use. Plans had to be made for handing over tools and other useful equipment to the military should an invasion occur.

The prime focus of the emergency scheme was to ensure that the military could respond in the event of invasion and that the civilian population would effectively aid the military and know what to do. Initially, the view taken was that in an invasion, people from nearer the coast would be evacuated or flee into this area. Lists were drawn up across the County of special constables, scouts and others able to help with the various tasks required.

The Central Committee was chaired by Samuel Howard Whitbread and included Major Frank Stevens, the Chief Constable. The Local Emergency Committees included the Bedford County Emergency Committee, which covered several villages in the Bedford area, including Willington, and was chaired by Walter Harter, a County Councillor. He in turn placed Willington, Cople, Cardington, Eastcotts, Wilstead and Elstow under the control of J. Arnold Whitchurch. In keeping with this structure, the role of special constable in Willington was allocated to Isaac Godber. He was required to appoint four men to take charge of livestock, tools, transport and food stuff[11]. Arrangements were made for livestock to be rendered unfit for consumption or driven to a designated collection point should the order be given. Saws, axes, ropes, picks and spades were to be ready for transporting to a designated centre for military use. Plans were made for food stuff to be destroyed or collected as and when required. Motor vehicles were also to be ready for assembling at a designated point.

Air raids became an issue with bombing raids on England by Zeppelin airships from 1915 and by Gotha bombers from 1917. These raids provoked calls for reprisals and a determination not to give in on the one hand and anxiety and concern on the other. Bedfordshire special constables and emergency special constables were directed, once the 'Take Air Raid Action' order was given, to ensure house and vehicle lights were out with only authorised vehicles allowed to travel with lights. Isaac Godber took on the role of emergency special constable for Willington, working with two special constables. When the order was in effect, he had to stand on duty at the junction of the Moggerhanger and Great Barford roads and await orders. In the end, this task turned out to be precautionary, and while it involved being called out at all hours in response to air raid alarms, actual raids did not target the village.

In fact, however, air raids were too close for comfort. Bessie Godber described one alarm in an undated letter to her sister:

> *"No. I didn't see the Zeppelin but had gone off to sleep and the pheasants in Sheerhatch wood woke me – they made such a row – so I got out of bed, thinking it was people cheering, but there was nothing to see then. However, Ike saw it, he was out up the village and came down just after and told me, so I put my dressing gown on, threw up the window and sat there a bit and presently I heard a droning noise getting louder and it was another Zep that sailed across from the east and disappeared from hearing (I didn't see it – it was too far away – probably 6 miles at the nearest) almost directly. I saw some bright flashes and then heard bombs exploding, quite a lot one after another and then nothing more … we also heard some bombs dropped in the direction of Northampton. It made me feel rather quakey*

and wondering how many poor souls had been done to death – but luckily not many this time."

Figure 12: advertisement inspired by the Zeppelin raids

The Biggleswade Chronicle also reported how local people were very much aware of the raids and how Londoners came to the area to get away from them. This is seen in reports on October 5th and October 26th, 1917:

"A good deal of interest has been aroused nearly every evening for more than a week, in the lights that could be seen in a

southerly and south-easterly direction. A good deal of discussion has resulted as to whether these lights were star shells or rockets or shell sparks. The sound of guns and bombs was heard very plainly on Sunday and Monday in the town and surrounding villages … The recent London air raids have brought us many visitors during the week."

"During the Zeppelin air raid on Friday evening last, reports of explosions were distinctly heard at Sandy."

The basic emergency plans set out early in the War remained in place. However, in August 1916 they were modified to the effect that 'in the event of a hostile landing, it will not be necessary to destroy or remove foodstuffs and stock.' The view now was that it would 'not be desirable that the civil population should be removed from areas occupied or likely to be occupied by the enemy.' The emergency arrangements were finally ended by the Home Office in December 1918 and, of course, while there had been bombing raids elsewhere, there had not been an invasion.

Directions under DORA were also given for how land was to be used to support the war effort. The German U-boat campaign to target merchant ships bringing supplies to Britain escalated and became unrestricted in 1917. The response was to increase the home production of grain by bringing more land into arable use. In Willington, this can be seen at Hill Farm, where grassland previously used for livestock was subjected to a ploughing order and to be used to grow crops. This did not go smoothly. The tenant at Hill Farm, William Brooks put in a claim for compensation to the Bedfordshire Agricultural Executive Committee citing the costs of ploughing, saying he had had to sell some of his cows and sheep as he could no longer grow enough feed and buying it in was costly. He argued that late ploughing due to the timing of the order and insect attacks had led to the failure of newly planted crops. He claimed compensation of £787 4s 0d but in the end settled in 1920 for £154. During the correspondence about his claim, he complained of 'shortness of labour' and tried to obtain permission to get a former farmhand back from the Front. He also mentioned having to suspend work due to the danger from firing on a nearby range[12]. It must be pointed out, however, that across the country, the move to convert pasture land to arable use did lead to an increase in grain production, which helped to reduce the impact of the U-boat campaign.

This was all very different from previous conflicts. Total war involved everyone in some way and the chairman of W.H. Allen commented that 'the War has altered everything.'[13]

Village Life and Work

In Willington, not quite everything altered. The Willington Parish Council still had routine matters to deal with, rejecting the need for additional workmen's dwellings and dealing with drainage problems and flooding caused by a blockage to the piped drain in Station Road. They also opposed a proposed move of early closing at the Willington Post Office from Saturday to Thursday as this would inconvenience market gardeners.

There are reports of local crimes and incidents that reflect the normal vicissitudes of Willington village life. In April 1915, William Brooks, mentioned above, was sentenced to a fine of £2 or one month in prison for failing to notify the authorities of a horse with mange[14]. The November 9th, 1917 *Bedfordshire Times and Independent* reported cases at the Bedford Petty Sessions. Several cyclists had been caught riding without lights in Willington and were fined. There was also the case of one villager, George Jakings, a carpenter, accused of killing four partridges at Cardington without a licence. He was said to have got off his bicycle, assembled a double-barrelled gun and shot at the partridges from behind a hedge. He was fined £5 with costs of 11/6d. He had previously been in trouble for a similar offence committed near Willington station. A more serious incident was reported in the same newspaper on May 26th, 1916. This took place at Willington station and concerned the death of eighteen-year-old Frank Barcock; he was run over by a train, which unexpectedly moved off, while he was trying to remove a sheet hanging over the wheels of one of the wagons.

Attempts were made to give the children as normal a Christmas as possible. There is a report in 1915 of a children's tea and Christmas tree party on Boxing Day given in the village school room. Tea was served, and presents were given out from around the tree, which a local farmer had provided. Books were given to the older children and toys, dolls and pencil cases to the younger ones. Isaac Godber acted as master of ceremonies and his wife, Bessie, gave out the presents. The War must have receded briefly during these festivities.

Despite these aspects of normality, the alterations to village life during the War were dramatic. People had to contend with the fluctuating emotions of relief, anxiety and heartbreak as news arrived from the Front. As noted, fund raising, making items for the troops and implementing emergency measures, occupied a good deal of time and energy. There was the wide range of restrictions and regulations imposed under DORA. Economies had to be made; for example, clothes had to last longer, and thrift was encouraged. Food became more expensive, prices came to be controlled, food shortages occurred, and rationing came in. Labour became scarce as men left to fight and jobs had to be filled in different ways.

Keeping farms, market gardens and nurseries going could be challenging. After conscription came in, some men gained at least temporary exemption from joining up on the grounds they were working full time, doing essential work on the land. Nevertheless, the existing labour shortage worsened. Farmers, market gardeners and nurserymen became increasingly dependent not only on those excused from military service, but also on women, schoolboys, prisoners of war and, when they were available, locally based soldiers detailed to work on the land. The following comments from Joyce Godber shed some light on the situation as it affected Willington:

> *"Labour position was desperate - no thought of keeping key men on the land and tomatoes were not recognised as food till towards the end of the war ... The sons[15] were called at 6 am, had to do an hour's work on farm or nursery before coming in to breakfast and change for school! Owen Williamson, who on being wounded was transferred to Labour Corps and came to work on nursery."*

Various steps were taken to ease the labour shortage. To facilitate the use of schoolboys in agriculture, the County Education Committee instructed the Director of Education in January 1915 not to enforce school attendance on boys over 12 years of age if they were employed in agricultural work due to the shortage of labour caused by the War. Later, in November 1916, a substitution scheme was promoted by the military authorities. Under this scheme, farmers and small holders were offered substitutes in the shape of men in the army, who were not fit for general service, in exchange for sound men employed on the land or in other occupations.

In 1917, military help was formalised with the formation of the Labour Corps. This was intended to provide a more efficient way of organising the support needed for the War. The men involved were typically not fit enough or too old for frontline service or had been wounded, like Owen Williamson, who had previously served in the Machine Gun Corps and had become lame. Seven of the Willington men[16] who served in the War joined the Labour Corps at some point. Those serving overseas in the Labour Corps built and repaired roads, railways and defences, laid cables, moved supplies, looked after services for soldiers taking rest from the Front and buried the dead. Those in the United Kingdom served at military bases, hospitals and factories or in the Labour Corps Agricultural Companies, working on the land.

There are also examples of men being discharged to the reserve and allowed to return to do vital work on the land. Two examples from Willington were James (Jimmy) Freeston and Edward Golder, who were both discharged in 1917 to work as steam ploughmen for Mr N.J.Hull of Bedford.

Significantly, the War also led to women taking up jobs previously done by men. This was something very much encouraged by the Government with the aim of releasing men to go and fight or to fill jobs men had vacated. Spurred on by the shell shortage of 1915, Lloyd George led the call for women to work in munitions factories, such as the Queen's Engineering Works of W.H. Allen in Bedford. Throughout the War and especially after conscription, women took up a wide range of jobs, working on the land, in offices, in shops, as drivers and conductors and so on. This was portrayed as 'doing your bit' but, as was the case with men, who volunteered to fight, patriotism appears to have been just one of a range of motives.

In Bedfordshire work on the land required female labour. Consequently, in February 1916, in line with practice across the country, the Women's War Agricultural Committee for Bedfordshire was set up, chaired by Madeline Whitbread. The County was divided into fourteen districts with one woman appointed as registrar in each parish. Bessie Godber became registrar for Willington. Her role was to maintain a register of women willing to work on the land and deal with applications for female workers[17]. In March 1916 an eight-week training scheme for women on approved farms was announced by the County Council, one of several approaches to training put in place. Despite these efforts, prejudice against women working on the land remained. To encourage farmers to use women, an agricultural demonstration and competition was held at Biddenham in June 1916.

Figure 13: the farming demonstration at Biddenham, designed to encourage the employment of women on farms

This featured competitions with women managing calves, horses and driving stock, ploughing, milking, hoeing, weeding and planting root vegetables, and attracted a good deal of interest. The report of the event indicated some of the prejudices the event had set out to overcome:

> *"These girls were doing their best in the midst of a multitude of agricultural experts and critics, to show that they could be of service to the farm and to the country, and they were endeavouring to disarm the criticisms and ridicule with which that proposition has been assailed. It was very plucky of them to make the attempt."*

While the standard in the various competitions was deemed to have varied, the event was considered a success and prizes were presented by Madeline Whitbread. The article covering the event[18] points out though that while many women were employed in market gardening, farm work had not been taken up to the same extent.

The wages books of Isaac Godber show an increase in the number of women he employed in Willington as the War progressed:

Date	Men employed	Women employed	Men's pay including insurance	Women's pay including insurance	Total wage bill
w/e 7/8/1914	21	9	£16 6s 1d	£2 2s 5d	£18 8s 6d
w/e 6/8/1915	18	10	£12 5s 11d	£2 9s 3d	£14 15s 2d
w/e 4/8/1916	11	18	£11 7s 6d	£10 2s 5d	£21 9s 11d
w/e 3/8/1917	10	11	£11 16s 11½d	£3 10s 2½d	£15 7s 2d

Figure 14: employment and wages in Willington among the workers of Isaac Godber

In a report on Women's Labour of December 1916, produced by the Women's War Agricultural Committee after conscription was introduced, it was estimated that 2200 women in the County worked on the land 'of whom 525 are regular workers and the remaining 1675 are employed casually.' The report indicated that it had been the custom for many years for women to work in market gardening and that many of the casual workers were employed in that way.

The position in Willington by December 1916 was that five women were regularly employed and ten were casually employed. Apart from these women, there were five more registered as available for work on the land in Willington and a further forty women who were unregistered. The following comment summarised the overall position in the Bedford East district, that included Willington:

> "Employment of women varied very much in the district according to whether market garden stuff is grown as at Gt Barford and Willington or whether it is ordinary arable farming. In Wilden and Ravensden most of the women help with poultry and other light work, but the land is too heavy for the average woman's capabilities." [19]

The situation was formalised and taken up a level in March 1917 with the formation across the country of the Women's Land Army to which women aged 18 and above could sign up. Their commitment was to a year's National Service in agriculture, foraging or timber cutting. The rationale was that:

> "Every woman who helps in agriculture during the war is as truly serving her country as the man who is fighting in the trenches or on the sea." [20]

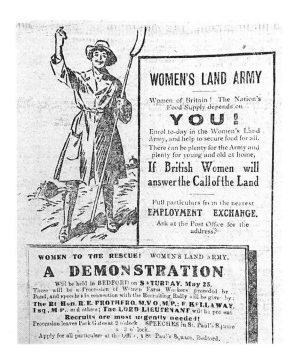

Figure 15: advertisement for the Land Army

The scheme was publicised and promoted, and the infrastructure of registrars created previously was used to take it forward. Measures were taken to provide training and to test the skills of working with cows and horses, ploughing and general labouring. There is, in fact, a record of a visit to Grange Farm, Willington, by the inspector as he went about the County conducting these efficiency tests on working members of the Women's Land Army. He came to see the daughter of Mark Young's bailiff. Her name is, perhaps tellingly, not given in his record of the visit and he found that she was 'not sufficiently capable for entering a horse work test.'[21].

Most of the women recruited to the Women's Land Army worked on farms or on market gardens as opposed to foraging or cutting timber[22]. Those joining were feted and recognised for their efforts, and rallies organised by the Women's War Agricultural Committee were held for the Bedfordshire members of the Land Army, such as one attended by 50 women and reported in Bedford in January 1918[23]. The Land Army was finally disbanded in 1919.

Overall there had been more success in getting Bedfordshire women involved in market gardening, a traditional form of female employment, than on farms, where prejudice against women workers persisted. In addition, as the War came to an end, the dominant view was that a woman should relinquish her job to a returning soldier.

In these ways, attempts were made to balance the needs of fighting the War with feeding the population. As can be seen, the attempts were not without problems, and frustrations continued throughout the War. There was criticism in the area that those working on the land, and exempt from military service, were being made to practise drill at the end of a long and hard day's work[24]. It was noted in June 1918 that:

> "farmers and market gardeners everywhere are complaining of the shortage of labour and the military authorities have no further supply at present of soldiers who can be employed on the land."[25]

Frustration can also be seen in the following comments in the Biggleswade Chronicle of July 19th, 1918:

> "the muddle as to the agricultural worker seems to continue ... no one appears to understand how an agriculturist stands with regard to military service."

Towards the end of the War, after several other measures controlling the price and provision of food, feeding bread to horses or chickens was banned and rationing came in. Bessie Godber commented on the impact of rationing in an undated letter to her sister:

> "How do you get on with your rationing? Meat and sugar, we can keep well within limits, but bread and flour are another matter – we certainly overstep the mark there, our children alone eat a loaf for tea, and they have never liked milk puddings, but I make one every other day now."

In the end, a key factor in the Allied victory was that both their civilian and military populations had been fed better than those of their enemies. Willington and the rest of Bedfordshire had played their part.

Soldiers at the Front

We now turn to the experiences of the Willington men who served, starting with those on the Western Front, the key battleground of the War. Here Germany counted on a quick victory before turning to fight Russia. The German plan failed and both sides dug in for four years of trench warfare. Soldiers' experience here varied depending on whether they were in an active or quiet sector. In any case, soldiers in combat roles alternated time behind the lines with spells in the front line. Being in the wrong place at the wrong time was a matter of chance.

Figure 16: a soldier's cartoon about leaving Bedford

Not surprisingly, the first Willington casualty of the War occurred on the Western Front. This was Private Ernest Bartram of the 2nd Battalion, Grenadier Guards who was killed in action on September 14th, 1914 in the battle of the Aisne. Ernest Bartram, listed as a farm labourer in the 1911 census, was in a regular army battalion that arrived in France as part of the British Expeditionary Force in August 1914.

Figure 17: soldiers of the Bedfordshire Regiment returning to the Front after recovering from wounds

The Battalion fought at Mons, the Marne and on the Aisne, in the battles that effectively ended the German plan for a quick victory in the west. They led to both sides digging themselves in and the

stalemate of trench warfare. The Battalion war diary for the day
Ernest Bartram died reads as follows:

> "14th Sep 1914. Advance at 05:30 and crossed the River Aisne at
> Gout Arey by pontoon bridge. Division engaged Battalions took
> and held position near Farm La Coeur De Soupir. Heavily
> engaged. Lost 2 Officers killed … 6 Officers wounded … and
> NCOs and men as follows: - 17 killed, 67 wounded 77 missing.
> Battalion entrenched and remained in Battle outpost positions
> already taken."[26]

The next Willington casualty on the Western Front, George Franklin,
was born in Northill and had lived in Sandy. He joined the
Bedfordshire militia in 1904, served in the military for eight years
before the War and was a reservist when the conflict began. As such,
he was among the first to be mobilised and served with the 1st
Battalion, Bedfordshire Regiment.

This Battalion was made up of regular soldiers and reservists and
formed part of the British Expeditionary Force in August 1914. They
had a torrid time fighting in the first engagements of the War on the
Western Front. In 1915, they were engaged in the Second Battle of
Ypres, fighting at Hill 60, also known as 'Murder Hill.' Later the
Battalion fought at the Battle of the Somme in 1916, and at Arras
and the Third Battle of Ypres in 1917, before moving briefly to the
Italian Front in December 1917. In April 1918, they came back to

France and remained on the Western Front until the end of the War[27]. Three other Willington men, Edgar Swannell, (who was killed in 1918 and is referred to below), Charles Sharman and John Webb are recorded as being in the 1st Battalion, Bedfordshire Regiment. A few other Willington men are simply listed as in the Bedfordshire Regiment without a battalion being specified.

A letter[28] from George Franklin to his father appeared in the Biggleswade newspaper on January 29th, 1915 under the heading *'Lucky Sandy Soldier.'* It had been sent from No 5, Base Hospital, Rouen:

> *"Dear Father, Just a few lines hoping to find you quite well in health as it leaves me at present, but I have stopped a bit of shell in my thigh, but it is going on alright. Glad to say it was the last shell the Germans fired that afternoon, the 16th. The same shell killed the Captain and two men. I was talking to the Captain at the time. So you see I must have been lucky. It wounded two more beside me. They shelled our trenches for an hour. I must say it's alright in here. A good bed to lie on, so it seems a treat after coming out of the trenches. I have not been out of bed yet. I don't mind this for a little time. The sisters and doctors are very kind and good to us."*

In fact, as well as the Captain, four men from the regiment were killed and eleven were wounded on that day. George Franklin recovered and returned to the Front. On April 23rd, 1915, the Bedford newspaper quoted part of another letter from him:

"You will be glad to know that I have recovered from the effects of my wound and am again in the firing line. We are having it 'hot' just now. Most of the fighting is in the woods, which prove a good mark for the German artillery, but, of course, we have the same advantage over them. You ought to hear our Artillery 'letting forth'. I think it is doing some good now. It seems impossible for the enemy to advance against our rifle fire. I think we have them in hand now."

On June 18th, 1915, the Biggleswade Chronicle reported he had been killed in action on May 5th, based on a letter to his father from his comrade, Lance Corporal R. Eaton, (who became a sergeant and survived the War). The report refers to him as Corporal William George Franklin, aged 28 and son of Mr W. Franklin of Willow Hill Cottages, Willington. The letter dated May 31st breaking the news of his death reads as follows:

"Dear Mr. and Mrs Franklin, it is with deep regret that we should have to write these few lines to break the sad news of your son's death, who was killed in action on the 5th inst. I am sure we deeply sympathise with you in your great loss. Speaking as a comrade, he left nothing to be desired. The Captain said: 'We have lost a good soldier and one of the best N.C.Os in the Coy.' I have been with your son from the start, and there could have been none braver than he shown himself on Hill 60, when they called for a volunteer to collect ammunition under heavy shell and rifle fire, he was one of the first to step forward, whilst he was also mentioned in despatches and would eventually be awarded the D.C.M. [Distinguished Conduct Medal.] *His was a painless death, as he was killed outright, whilst doing his duty. I*

come from Sandy and have known him all my life. I remain, yours truly, R. Eaton."

A memorial service was held in the church and in due course, George Franklin was awarded the medal of the Order of St George, 4th class, a Russian decoration (rather than the D.C.M.), in recognition of his gallant conduct in the field. On the medal citation he was referred to as Acting Corporal. He was one of two men with a Willington connection to be awarded a gallantry medal[29].

The war diary for the 1st Battalion, Bedfordshire Regiment gives an indication of the fierce fighting on the day George Franklin died:

"May 5th: The night passed very quietly, only occasional shots were fired from the trenches in front of us. Usually the Germans fired a great number of 'very [sic] lights' [flares] each night but very few had been fired during the night. The enemy's quietness rather disturbed us for he was always quiet just before battle. We had not long to wait after daylight before we learnt what the enemy's intentions were. A little before 8 a.m. he discharged gas from two points opposite the Battalion front. One of these points was immediately in front of our trench; the trenches here were less than a hundred yards apart. We could see the gas being pumped out above their trench. It travelled over our lines being carried gently along by a light breeze.

At the same time as the gas was discharged our trenches and Battery positions were subject to an appalling bombardment by the enemy's heavy guns. The alarm was sounded and the S.O.S. signal sent by phone to the Artillery who replied at once with a heavy fire on the German frontline. The signal to the Artillery got through just in time as all lines were reported broken immediately afterwards.

German infantry were observed in the trenches opposite massing for an attack, in fact their trenches were crowded, some of them mounted the parapets to attack but they got no further. Our men put up such a rapid and well directed fire that the German infantry simply melted away. Nearly all our men were by this time suffering from the effects of gas, but this did not stop them from firing their rifles.

The troops on our right, however, were driven out of their trenches or overcome by gas, and Hill 60 was captured by the enemy. A very desperate struggle went on all day. On our right, the enemy having obtained a footing in the trenches on Hill 60 worked outwards and eventually got through the gap on our right but were then held by our right Company who gallantly maintained their positions.

The enemy having been repulsed on our front now settled down to blow us out of our trenches with heavy guns, and trench mortars, and for the remainder of the day subjected us to an intense bombardment. A bomb from a heavy trench mortar exploded in the trench among a section of my platoon and killed every man, and two signallers who were operating a telephone. The number of men killed by this mortar was 15.

Towards evening reinforcements were sent up by the 13th Infantry Brigade and a counter attack was made on Hill 60, but they failed to retake the Hill.

Our casualties during the day were very heavy. Captain Gladstaines [Arthur Sheldon Gledstanes] *was severely wounded and died next day, Lieut Hopkins was killed and Lieut Whittemore wounded. The casualties amongst other ranks were: killed or died of wounds or gas poisoning 48. Wounded and admitted to hospital from the effects of gas 250."[30]*

The Commonwealth War Graves Commission (CWGC) database has George Franklin as a Corporal with the date of death as June 5th, 1915. This appears to be a mistake, given the letter quoted above, and the fact that June 5th was an uneventful day according to the Battalion war diary. According to the CWGC, he is commemorated on the Menin Gate in Ypres; his parents are listed as William and Lucy Franklin of 7 George Town, Sandy. This misses the fact his father had moved and remarried by the time of George's death.

There is evidence here of the difficulty of producing precise up-to-date information amid the fog of war. This example also illustrates the issues in deciding where to commemorate those who served. People sometimes had connections with more than one place before the War or their next of kin had moved, both of which happened in this case. Indeed, George Franklin is commemorated in Willington, Moggerhanger and Sandy. This is understandable given that George grew up in Sandy and his father, at the time George died, lived on the road between Willington and Moggerhanger.

Another soldier to have a letter quoted in the Bedford newspaper was Fred Cooper, who had been a farm labourer before the War. He too saw service on the Western Front. A letter from him to his mother was referred to on March 24th, 1916. Fred Cooper is listed as a corporal in the Parish Council Minutes and served initially with the 6th Battalion, Bedfordshire Regiment.

In the letter he told his mother that he and Harry were keeping well and safe, and went on to say:

"We have had a very rough day today. The Germans have been shelling us all day, but they have not hurt many of us. They have just left off, so I feel a bit more like writing a letter now than I did when those bits of iron were flying about us. I think we are going back on Friday for our rest, and we are pleased to hear it. I think the people in England don't know the 6th Bedfords are out here, but never mind, we can stick it. We think it would do some of them good to come out here and do a bit; we can make room for them in the 6th Bedfords."

Figure 18: Fred Cooper

We get a hint here of some resentment that not everyone was doing their bit. The letter points to a gulf developing between soldiers and those at home. The 6th Battalion, Bedfordshire Regiment was raised in August 1914 in response to Lord Kitchener's call for men to volunteer to fight for their country. The Battalion fought on the Western Front throughout the War, including at the Battle of the Somme in 1916.

According to the 1918 Absent Voters' Register, Fred Cooper later moved to the Agricultural Labour Corps, presumably after he was wounded in the knee. He survived the War. The 'Harry' Fred referred to was most probably Harry Hayden, who died from wounds during the Battle of the Somme on August 21st, 1916.

In August 1917 confirmation came of the death of another Willington man, Private Robert Webb, aged 30, the only son of Levi and Annie E. Webb. Before the War, he had worked as a nursery labourer. He had been missing since October 23rd, 1916 but had now been officially confirmed as dead on that date. He had served first with the South Staffordshire Regiment and then with the 1st Battalion, Royal Warwickshire Regiment. He died on the Western Front in the later stages of the Somme offensive, one of 57,722 British soldiers killed in the month of October.

The 1916 Somme offensive had been designed to enable the Allies to win the War through simultaneous attacks on the Eastern and Western Fronts. There had been pressure from the French to commit and Kitchener's New Armies were put to the test.

The Allied strategy was undermined by the German attack at Verdun in late February 1916, which drew the French away and by differences over whether the aim was to break through the German lines or wear down their defences. In the end, troops got bogged down in the mud, and while the offensive drained German resources, the cost to the Allies in manpower and resources was equally heavy. Nevertheless, important lessons were learned, and experience was gained.

Tragedy struck more than once in the same family in the case of William and Arthur Golder of Willington, both killed in April 1917. As noted above, a memorial service was held for them in the church. Private William Golder was in the 11th Battalion, Middlesex Regiment and was killed in action on the Western Front on April 9th, 1917. He had formerly been in the Royal Fusiliers. The 11th Battalion was formed in 1914 for the duration of the War in response to Kitchener's call for volunteers. The Battalion fought at the Battle of Loos in 1915, on the Somme in 1916 and in the Arras offensive in 1917[31]. The date recorded for William Golder's death was the first day of the Arras offensive and judging from the deployment of his Battalion, this would have been at the First Battle of the Scarpe. Over the three days of this battle, casualties numbered 13,000, but lessons had been learnt from previous battles and the advances were the furthest of the War to that point in time[32].

William Golder was born in Oxfordshire but later moved with his family to Willington and married. He and his wife, Ada, lived on the Bedford Road. In the 1911 census, he is listed as a milk salesman and as having two young sons. He was 36 at the time of his death.

William's brother, Private Arthur Golder, was killed in Salonica on April 28th, 1917 and we will look at what happened to him later after discussing other Willington men who fought on the Western Front.

In addition to the fatalities in 1917 mentioned above, George Clarke of the 8th Battalion, Seaforth Highlanders died at the battle of Ypres and George Dawks of the 1st Battalion, Cambridgeshire Regiment was killed together with sixty-one of his comrades in an attack on a German stronghold called Joist Redoubt in the Ypres salient.

In Spring 1918, the Germans launched a series of offensives to try to break the stalemate on the Western Front. The aim was to strike before the arrival of the American army could make a difference. The attacks made use of troops freed up after peace was made with

Russia following the 1917 revolution. Some Willington men died resisting the German advances. Frederick Herbert Stokes of Willington died on the Western Front on March 28th, 1918. He was with the 7th Battalion, Queen's Own Royal West Kent Regiment. In the week leading up to his death, his regiment had taken heavy casualties as they fought against the German offensive in the Oise region of France.

Figure 19: British soldiers occupying a German trench

In May 1918, news came of the death of Private Daniel Gudgin of the 9th Battalion, Essex Regiment. This regiment was created in 1914 in response to Kitchener's call for volunteers and landed in France in

1915. Daniel Gudgin was killed in action on the Western Front on April 5th, 1918. His regiment was in the Hénencourt area of the department of the Somme in the thick of the German offensive. On the day he died, his regiment came under attack beginning with an intense artillery bombardment. He is listed in the 1911 census as a labourer on a nursery but had gone on to be a porter at the Bedford Midland Road Railway Station. He was the son of Henry and Julia Gudgin of Barford Road.

One Willington man, remembered in a memorial service in the church, was Private Edgar Swannell of the 1st Battalion, Bedfordshire Regiment. He was killed in action on the Western Front in the Nieppe Forest on May 12th, 1918, aged 24. He and his fellow soldiers appear to have been involved in improving the trenches and laying down barbed wire in the first days of May, a reminder of the routine tasks soldiers faced in maintaining their defences. They had faced very active enemy machine gun fire from the 10th. Edgar's parents, Robert and Charity, lived in Hill Farm Cottages in Willington. They had previously lived in Felmersham, where Edgar was born. Before the War, according to the 1911 census, he had been a farm labourer.

Another fatality was reported in the Bedford newspaper on July 5th, 1918 in the Gamlingay notes. This was Herbert Ray of the 2nd Battalion, Suffolk Regiment, who had previously served with the

Royal Garrison Artillery (RGA). Herbert Ray was killed in action on June 15th, 1918 on the Western Front in the Pas de Calais area. The regimental diary indicates that his regiment came under heavy shelling and machine gun fire that day and that three men were killed and five were wounded. He is listed as private in the newspaper and on the Willington war memorial but as a corporal on the CWGC database. The letter breaking the news of his death was printed in the Cambridge Daily news on July 4th, 1918:

> *"It is with a sad heart, that I have to tell you that your son was killed in action on the night of the 15th June. His death was instantaneous, so he suffered no pain. The officers and N.C.O's and men of this company miss him immensely as he was greatly admired by all who knew him for his courage and gallantry. This must be a bitter blow to you all. Please accept my deepest sympathy to you and yours on your great loss."*

By the time of his death, aged 24, his parents, Thomas and Ellen Jane Ray, were living in Willington at 5, Church Road. However, they had previously lived in High Road, Gamlingay with Herbert as indicated in the 1911 census return. Both father and son were farm labourers. Herbert Ray was named on the Gamlingay war memorial as well as on the Willington memorials. Like George Franklin, he was commemorated in more than one of the places, where his family lived.

The German Spring attacks were successful at first but by August 1918, the Germans were driven back, outnumbered in terms of both men and armaments. Faced with unrest and economic hardship at home, the collapse of their allies and an exhausted army, Germany accepted defeat and on November 11th an armistice was signed. Attention now turned to determining peace terms.

For some Willington men, the War involved carrying out the support, reconnaissance and logistical tasks required by the army. Among these was Harry Spavins, who served with the Royal Engineers Signal Service. Because of his previous experience as a telegraphist at his mother's Post Office in the village, he carried out reconnaissance, signalling details of enemy positions from hot air balloons. The Willington men with the Army Service Corps (ASC)[33] maintained and operated the transport links to the Western and other front lines. One of those with the ASC was Walter William Weedon, who qualified to drive heavy lorries and is named on the village war memorials. The ASC medal roll shows he transferred from the 1st Rifle Battalion to the ASC in November 1917 and was discharged from the ASC on May 7th, 1919 as no longer fit for military service. He died of heart disease on May 26th, aged 38, at the Gables in Willington, the home of his sister and brother-in-law. During the War he had gone from being passed as A1 on joining up to terminally ill, a reflection of either the cursory medical inspections for new recruits or of unhealthy living conditions. No grave or memorial is listed for him on the CWGC database.

One aspect of the eventual peace settlement was the creation of a demilitarised zone in the Rhineland to act as a buffer between Germany and France. Troops were stationed there to police it. A Willington man, Private Sidney Victor Cross died there on January 23rd, 1920. The Parish Council Minutes indicate he was killed by accident while on foreign service. He had been a mechanic before being called up. At the time of his death, he was with what by then had become the *Royal* Army Service Corps Motor Transport Department (Rhine) and is buried in Cologne Southern Cemetery. The date of Victor's death is a reminder that there was no swift return home for troops after the armistice and that danger still existed. His widow, Daisy received some money from the Army, which also invested money on his behalf in National Savings Certificates for her and their daughter, Gwendoline.

From these examples, we can get an insight into what the War involved for some of the Willington men who served on the Western Front, with its battles of attrition and pushes for a breakthrough. The experience was a mixture of boredom, squalor, camaraderie, fear, fatalism and bravery. Days for combat troops in the front line were outnumbered by days of training, digging, repairing defences, waiting and recuperation. Although the examples given above have mainly focused on those who died, others, of course, survived, sometimes with wounds, and returned home after the War was over.

Three Willington men, Walter Ashwell, Arthur Golder and Leonard Purser died fighting around the Mediterranean. For the Germans, the aim in this area was to divert British forces from the Western Front by threatening Britain's links to India, then part of the British Empire. To do this meant influencing and supporting the war plans of Germany's ally, the Ottoman Empire. Britain was concerned to safeguard her position in India and with attacking Germany's allies, Bulgaria, Austria-Hungary and the Ottoman Empire. Doing this created an opportunity for diverting German troops away from the Western Front.

Walter Ashwell was with the 4th Battalion, South Wales Borderers and died on September 8th, 1917. His Battalion saw action around the Mediterranean from 1915, when they landed in Gallipoli and fought at the battle of Suvla Bay. The Battalion subsequently moved to Egypt and were then involved in the campaign against the Ottoman Empire in Mesopotamia (now Iraq). Walter Ashwell is commemorated on the Willington and Moggerhanger war memorials as well as on the one in Basra in the area where he died.

Figure 20: photograph of Bedfordshire soldiers in Egypt

As noted previously, Arthur Golder died in Salonica on April 28th, 1917 fighting against the Bulgarian army. He was in the 9th Battalion, King's Own Royal Lancashire Regiment, twenty-one years old and unmarried. His Battalion was formed in 1914 in response to Kitchener's call for volunteers and was to exist for the duration of the War. The Battalion arrived in Salonica in November 1915 with the strategy of drawing away German troops from the Western Front. The deployment was also a reaction to the conquest of Serbia by Austria-Hungary and Bulgaria's entry into the War on the side of the Central Powers, based on the promise of land in the Balkans.

*Figure 21: Moggerhanger war memorial, with the names of
Walter Ashwell and George W. Franklin*

The Battalion was subsequently involved in several actions against

the Bulgarian army. In April and May 1917 came the Battle of Doiran

at which Arthur Golder was killed. This was an attempt to break

through the Bulgarian lines and divert more German forces to the

region. The British came up against well-coordinated defences and

the battle involved fierce fighting and heavy losses before ending in

failure. The British lost 12,000 men killed, wounded and captured

with more than 2,250 buried by the defenders[34]. Arthur is recorded

on the CWGC database as buried at Karasouli Military Cemetery,

Greece, a cemetery 'begun in September 1916 for the use of casualty

clearing stations on the Doiran Front'[35] with graves from other

cemeteries in the region transferred there later.

Arthur Golder was born in Willington and had been a farm labourer before he entered the War in 1916. His property of a wallet, a bible, a disc, a photograph and ten cards, was returned to his family. His family placed a death notice in the Bedford newspaper that contained a short poem:

> *"There's a lonely grave abroad*
> *Where our brave young hero sleeps.*
> *There's a cottage home in England*
> *Where his loved ones sit and weep.*
> *We think of him in silence*
> *And his name we oft recall,*
> *But there's nothing left to answer*
> *But his photo on the wall."*

Leonard Purser was with the 2/17th (2nd Stepney and Poplar Rifles) Battalion, London Regiment and died on May 2nd, 1918. His Battalion fought at the battle of Doiran in 1917, the battle in which Arthur Golder lost his life. They were then deployed against the Ottoman Empire, moving to Egypt and advancing into Palestine, where they took Jerusalem. Consequently, after his death, Leonard Purser was buried in the Jerusalem War Cemetery.

Records indicate that some others from Willington who survived the War fought around the Mediterranean. They include Claude Reginald Davison who fought in Mesopotamia, Albert Tom Hales who was in

Egypt and Frederick James Barcock, who was treated in hospital for malaria, and had been in Beirut and Alexandria.

Some ended the War serving in the Agricultural Labour Corps[36], possibly transferred there after being wounded or otherwise medically downgraded. They helped to ensure that adequate food supplies were available. In the end, as mentioned previously, winning the War depended very much on which of the powers could best feed and supply their civilians and their troops.

Each side tried to impose a naval blockade to create shortages of food and resources. German submarine (U-boat) attacks on merchant shipping were both a threat to the war effort and one of the factors that brought the USA into the War. One Willington man, Charles Dawson, was in the Royal Marine Light Infantry (R.M.L.I). He served on HMS Cumberland, which took part in Atlantic convoys, in which naval vessels escorted and protected groups of merchant ships. This system helped to combat the threat from what became unrestricted U-boat attacks on merchant shipping.

Overall, about twenty per cent of the 1911 Willington population of 370 served during the War. The overwhelming majority were in the army. The exceptions were Charles Dawson in the Royal Marine Light Infantry (R.M.L.I) and George Jakings who was in the RAF at the end of the War. The Willington war memorials in the Peace Memorial Hall and church each name the same sixteen men who died. Another man Private John Atkinson, who came from Great Barford but whose parents lived in Willington, served with the 8th Battalion, Bedfordshire Regiment and was killed on the Somme. The number of dead represents just over four per cent of the population of 1911 and slightly over twenty per cent of those who served[37]. By way of comparison with adjoining villages, ten per cent of the men who served from Cople died and thirty-eight per cent of those who served from Moggerhanger. To put this in context, it has been estimated that 71.5 million men were mobilised by all the countries involved in the War and that 9.5 million or just over thirteen per cent of them died. Twelve per cent of British and Irish soldiers died[38].

There were also the wounded and the sick. The official casualty lists and other surviving military records enable us to identify at least some of these. At least twelve Willington men survived gunshot or shrapnel wounds or were gassed. One of those wounded, Frank Gudgin, was also captured and taken to Germany as a prisoner of war, where he suffered from exposure and cold. Based on the records available, three men suffered from nephritis, two had trench feet, and others suffered respectively from trench fever, malaria, a hernia, an eye problem and vascular heart disease.

Given the changes to Willington before the War and the growth of the population, it is perhaps no surprise that not all those commemorated in the village were born or grew up in Willington. There are some gaps in the records, but it appears that only about one third of the men with a Willington connection who served were born in the village and just over half lived in the village at the time of the 1911 census. Four of the fallen were born in Willington and seven lived in the village when the 1911 census was taken.

After the War

As elsewhere, peace was celebrated in the village. Children in Willington and the rest of Bedfordshire were granted an extra week's holiday in summer 1919 in 'commemoration of Peace.' Plans were also made to commemorate the fallen and those who had served. Given delays in obtaining information and uncertainty about what had happened, there was some difficulty in arriving at a list of men to commemorate. This can be seen in the differences between the initial list inscribed in the minutes of the Parish Council and the lists on the village memorials that were installed subsequently.

On March 21st, 1920 there was an afternoon service in the church at which the village war memorial tablet was unveiled. The service was led by Rev Frederick Kingston and Rev George Whelpton, who had been the village's Methodist Minister for the latter part of the War. J. Arnold Whitchurch, a well-known local public figure, who played a key role in leading wartime emergency arrangements in the area and in the development of Bedford Hospital, unveiled the tablet.

Church of St. Lawrence, Willington,

March 21st, 1920.

In Memoriam.

WALTER ASHWELL.	FREDERIC CLARK.
JAMES DAWKES.	ERNEST BARTRAM.
HERBERT RAY.	HARRY HADEN.
WILLIAM FRANKLIN.	DANIEL GUDGIN.
WILLIAM GOLDER.	EDGAR SWANNELL.
ARTHUR GOLDER.	ROBERT WEBB.
WILLIAM WEEDON.	VICTOR CROSS.
LEONARD PURSER.	HERBERT STOKES.

Who gave their lives for their Country in the Great War.

Figure 22: order of service for the Willington memorial service[39]

The Vicar adapted Charlotte Elliott's nineteenth century hymn 'Just as I am' for the service. The following verse gives an indication of his approach:

"Just as they are! where no regard
Is in their eyes, their bodies scarred
With wounds and pitifully marred.
We leave them Lord with thee."

Understandably Kingston appears to have felt the impact of the War and the pain and loss it brought deeply. He had tried to bring what Christian comfort he could.

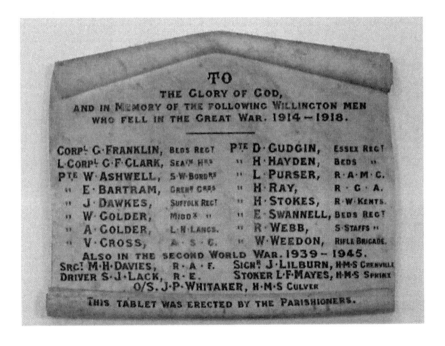

Figure 23: the war memorial tablet in St Lawrence Church, Willington

One initiative that had been largely put on hold during the War was the plan to build a village hall. Fund raising and planning for this resumed in earnest afterwards, causing a dispute between the Vicar and some of his parishioners over the use and investment of money and whether to have a temporary or permanent building.

Opposing views were exchanged verbally and in print, legal action was threatened, and the Vicar left the planning committee. In the end, the idea of a permanent building prevailed despite the Vicar's objections. The new hall opened in 1923 with the colours of what was then known as the Bedfordshire and Hertfordshire Regiment on display. The building was aptly named the Peace Memorial Hall, an idea originally suggested by the Vicar.

Figure 24: foundation stone of Willington Peace Memorial Hall dated
a year before the opening

The Peace Memorial Hall itself and the Roll of Honour and memorial board installed there were intended as a lasting and positive tribute to those who served. They marked a commitment to remember the men who died 'for God, King and Empire.' The words from the Book of Samuel on the Roll of Honour – 'they were a wall unto us both by day and night'[40] - recognised the debt that was felt.

However, hopes for a better world after the War were undermined by the slow pace of demobilisation, unemployment, poor diet, the physical and psychological damage caused by the War and the high expectations for what peace would bring. One man, Reginald Lymon, whose Willington uncle, Frank Barringer Spavins, served in the War, wrote:

> *"I remember that due to the War, and many years afterwards there seemed to be so few men about anywhere. So many had been killed and others had not yet been released from the services. Women were doing men's jobs everywhere in the fields and factories. Almost every day one would see more women appear dressed in deep black. They having been informed that their husband or other relative was presumed killed in France. I can picture my mother's brother, Uncle Frank, who incidentally spent four years in the trenches in France, coming home on leave and coming to see us in Tempsford. Like other men in the forces he had had his head shaved because of the lice and his clothes were all muddy and torn. Things were so bad that the army did not let them have a clean-up or clean clothes before they came home. He did survive the War but all his toes had*

been frozen off whilst lying in the dugouts. After the War he worked in the fields with his brother, my Uncle Syd, who had also returned from the War. He hardly ever spoke to anyone and spent his evenings in the pub and eventually went to pieces through drink. I particularly remember him because he showed me how to set fire to things with a magnifying glass as they used to do in France in the trenches. My, how these men suffered in the First World War."[41]

There were, of course, those who tried to do their bit to make the world a better place. One of these was Claude R. Davison. In the election to Sandy Parish Council in 1921, he 'offered himself as an ex-Service man after four and half years in the Army doing his duty for his King and country. He deplored the unemployment that existed. He had 40 ex-Service men in his employ and had never discharged one - if he hadn't work for them he made work.'[42] This expression of solidarity echoes the camaraderie often referred to when veterans reminisced. It represents a positive aspect of reactions to the War.

The First World War has been subject to extensive historical debate, not least on its centenary. As we consider the various interpretations, we can sometimes learn as much about a writer's outlook and present concerns as we can about the past. Some images from the time have become firmly fixed but not every day was spent knee deep in mud or going over the top. The stories presented in this book provide a means of testing out some of the generalisations about the War. As we have seen from this review of what happened to the people of Willington, chance played a part in whether a soldier survived, was wounded or died and in the kind of experience they had both during the conflict and afterwards. The village, like other parts of the country, had had to deal with the implications of total war for the first time in its history. While some aspects of life carried on as before, the War had a marked effect on both soldiers and civilians and for some, the impact stayed with them for the rest of their lives. Indeed, it appears to have shortened the lives of some of the soldiers who survived.

As we know, this was not a 'war to end wars.' Both for the country and the village, it provided experience that was drawn upon during the Second World War. There were links between the two wars involving people; men who had been soldiers in the First World War joined the Home Guard and organised fund raising for wartime causes in the Second World War. It was now their sons who served in the armed forces. Much as the First World War was a total war involving civilians as well as the military, so it was with the Second World War. Not surprisingly, therefore, there are strong parallels between what happened in the two wars.

Figure 25: Willington Peace Memorial Hall in the 1980s before recent alterations - as seen in a drawing in the foyer there

Figure 26: Willington Peace Memorial Hall Memorial Board

Appendix 1 – The Willington Roll of Honour in the Church

FOR·KING·AND·COUNTRY

THESE·WILLINGTON·MEN·

SERVED·IN·THE·GREAT·WAR·1914·1918

Cannon Cross
George M. Franklin
William Devonshire
Ernest Bartram
Percy Davidson
George Quince
Harry Haydon
Fredk Cooper
Edgar Swannell
Charles Wooding
Walter Purser
Charles Sharman
William Spavins
Arthur Usher
Albert Purser
A. Sidney Harding
Leslie Gammons
James Freeston
Frank Farr
George Martin
Frank W. Gudgin
William Purser
Charles Gammons
George F. Clarke
F. G. Clarke
Frank J. Barcock
Fred Barker
Chad Dawson
Alonzo J. Hall
Arthur Golder
Ernest Golder
Arthur Spavins
Cecil Sharman
Alfred Swannell

Frank Spavins
John Webb
Robert Webb
Joshua J. Sharman
Charles M. Dawson
William Golder
Percy Bartram
Walter Ashwell
Percy Harding
Albert Hales
George Lakings
Arthur Matthews
Harry Mayes
Frank Martin
Walter Norman
Leonard Purser
Herbert Spavins
George Usher
George Bartwell
William Meedon
Frederick Simmons
Daniel Gudgin
Edward J. Lack
Herbert Stokes
James Dawkes
Herbert Kay
Cecil Little
Herbert Norman
Ernest Matthews
Charles Chapman
Albert Robinson
William Boness
Victor Cross
Frank Cooper

The Red Capitals denote The Fallen.

78

Appendix 2 – Serving men with a Willington connection[43] † = died; * = not on Willington memorials

Rank, Name and Number	Comments
† Private Walter Ashwell 12101	In the 1911 census, he is listed as a farm labourer, living in Moggerhanger and was single. In the War, he was with the 4th Battalion, South Wales Borderers. He died on September 18th, 1917 in Turkey and is commemorated at the Basra Memorial, Iraq.
† Private John Atkinson* 17774	He was born in Blunham and lived in Great Barford, working as an agricultural labourer. He served with the 8th Battalion, Bedfordshire Regiment and was killed in action on the Somme on September 15th, 1916. He was the son of Mr and Mrs W.G. Atkinson of 3, Council Cottage, Willington, and a widower, aged 43 when he died. He is commemorated in Great Barford but not in Willington and buried in Serre Road Cemetery No 2.
Private Ernest Alonzo Ball 241479	In the 1911 census, he is listed as a farm labourer, living in Willington and was married. In the War, he was with the Bedfordshire Regiment and the 680 Agricultural Labour Corps.
Private Frederick James Barcock M2/177378	In the 1911 census, he is listed as a farm labourer, living in Willington and was single. When he joined in May 1916, he said he was a steam driver and served with the 955 Motor Transport ASC. He served in Middle East and caught malaria.
Sapper Frederick Barker 522470	In the War, he served with the 486 East Anglian (E.A.) Field Company Royal Engineers.
† Private Ernest Bartram 12799	In the 1911 census, he is listed as a farm labourer, living in Cople and was married. He served with the 2nd Battalion, Grenadier Guards and was killed in action on September 14th, 1914 on the Western Front at the battle of the Aisne. He is commemorated on the La Ferte-Sous-Jouarre Memorial.

Rank, Name and Number	Comments
Private Percy Bartram 33783	In the 1911 census, he is listed as a farm labourer, living in Willington and was single. He attested in December 1915 and joined up the following June. By then he was married with two children and was a steam ploughman. In the War he was with the 5th, 3rd, 8th and 2nd Battalions, Bedfordshire Regiment. He survived wounds while in action in the hand and legs in March and October 1918.
Private William George Boness 137285	This is the son of William James and Susan Boness from Sandy, who had moved to Road Farm, Willington by 1914. In the Parish Council minutes, he is recorded as having served with the Machine Gun Corps.
Private Charles Chapman	He is recorded as serving with the West Kent Regiment.
Private Frank E. Clarke	In 1911, he was possibly working as a baker and living in Kempston. He was married. He served with the 5th Royal Irish Lancers. His full name was listed as Francis Edward on the 1918 Willington Absent Voters' Register.
✝ Lance Serjeant George Frederick Clarke 94678/S10187	He served with the Royal Field Artillery and then with the 8th Battalion, Seaforth Highlanders and died of wounds on August 2nd, 1917 on the Western Front. He is recorded as a private by the Parish Council, lance corporal on the church memorial and as lance serjeant by CWGC; he died at the battle of Ypres and was buried at Lijssenthoek Military Cemetery.
Corporal Fred Cooper 17750/555133 Brother of Frank Redvers Cooper	In the 1911 census, he is listed as a farm labourer, living in Beeston and was single. He served with the 6th Battalion, Bedfordshire Regiment, (being wounded in the knee in June 1916), and 693 Agricultural Labour Corps. He was based in Willington and listed as a private on the 1918 Willington Absent Voters' Register.
Private Frank Redvers Cooper, Brother of Fred Cooper	In the 1911 census, he is listed as at school and as living in Beeston and was single. He served with the Suffolk Regiment and the Royal Sussex Regiment. He lived in Willington at the time of the 1921 Willington electoral register.

Rank, Name and Number	Comments
✝ Private Sidney Victor Cross M/317673	In the 1911 census, he is listed as a cycle and motor repairer, living in Willington and was single. By the time he joined up, he had married and had a daughter. He served with the RASC and was killed by accident on January 23rd, 1920 in Germany. He is buried in Cologne Southern Cemetery.
Gunner Cannon William Cross 35361 - Brother of Sidney Victor Cross	In the 1911 census, he is listed as a milk salesman, living in Willington and was single. In the War, he was with the 35 Heavy Battery, Royal Garrison Artillery.
Private Percy Davidson 161964	In the 1911 census, he is listed as a farm labourer, living in Cople and was single. In the War, he was with the Bedfordshire Regiment and the 5th Labour Unit. His name is spelled as Davison on the 1918 Willington Absent Voters' Register. He continued to live in the village and became a hydraulic engineer.
2nd Lt Claude Reginald Davison 1498	At the time of the 1911 census, he was at school living in Margate and single. According to the Biggleswade Chronicle (9/2/23), in the War "after joining the Beds. Yeomanry he, like so many others, from the late Colonel Shuttleworth's old volunteer mounted infantry regiment, gained a commission, and with King Edward's Horse, saw much service in France and Mesopotamia". He appears on the 1918 Willington Absent Voters' Register as a 2nd Lt in the Machine Gun Corps and is named on the Roll of Honour in the Peace Memorial Hall but not on that in the church. He followed his father, Frank Davison of Scarsdale, into farming, living at Southoe Manor, and died there in 1941, aged 46.

Rank, Name and Number	Comments
† Private George James Dawks 203907/41409 Brother-in-law of George William Franklin	In the 1911 census, he is listed at Willow Hill Farm in Moggerhanger and was a market gardening labourer. In the War, he was with the Bedfordshire Regiment and then with the Suffolk Regiment (1st Cambridgeshires). He died on September 26th, 1917 on the Western Front in an attack on Joist Redoubt. He married in Willington during the War and is listed on the 1918 Willington Absent Voters' Register. On some records, his name is spelled Dawkes. He is commemorated on the Tyne Cot Memorial.
Private Percy Dawson*	He served with the Bedfordshire Regiment but although on the 1918 Willington Absent Voters' Register is not on either Willington Roll of Honour.
Driver Ehud Irvine Dawson 522580/2397	In the 1911 census, he is listed as a horse boy on a farm in Willington and single. In the War, he was with the East Anglian Field Company, Royal Engineers, serving in France and ending the War in Stockheim, Germany. He is listed on the 1918 Willington Absent Voters' Register as Driver.
Private Charles William Dawson 18981 - Brother of Ehud Dawson	In the 1911 census, he was at school, living in Willington and single. He was a grocer's assistant on enlisting in June 1916, aged 17. He served on HMS Cumberland with the Royal Marine Light Infantry (R.M.L.I), staying on after the War.
Private William Charles Devonshire RX4/158253	In the 1911 census, he is listed as a coal carter, living in Willington and was married. In the War, he was with the Bedfordshire Yeomanry and the 49th Remount Squadron ASC.
Acting Corporal Frank Farr 8299	He came from Sandy, where he worked for Mark Young and joined the Bedfordshire militia in 1904. In the 1911 census, he is listed as a soldier in Bermuda and Jamaica. In the War, he served with the 2nd and 8th Battalions, Bedfordshire Regiment, going to France in 1914 and was wounded at the start of 1918. He is listed on the 1918 Willington Absent Voters' Register.

82

Rank, Name and Number	Comments
† Acting Corporal George William Franklin 8328 Brother-in-law of George James Dawks	He joined the Bedfordshire militia in 1904 on the same day as Frank Farr, giving his residence as Willow Hill, Moggerhanger, and stating he worked in market gardening for Frank Davison. In the 1911 census, he is listed as a soldier in Bermuda and Jamaica and single. In the War, he was with the 1st Battalion, Bedfordshire Regiment and killed in action on May 5th, 1915, fighting at Hill 60. He was awarded the medal of the Order of St George, 4th class. On the medal citation he was referred to as Acting Corporal. The CWGC database lists him as a corporal as do the two village Rolls of Honour. He is commemorated on the Menin Gate.
Driver James Thomas Freeston T3/O25282	In the 1911 census, he is listed as a carpenter and wheelwright from Leicestershire, living in Willington and single. In the War, he enlisted with the ASC as a wheelwright and went to France in December 1914. In 1916, he was treated for a broken arm, placed in the reserve in May 1917 and allowed to return to his pre-war job as a steam ploughman with Mr N.J. Hull of Bedford. He is listed in the 1918 Willington Absent Voters' Register; his name is spelled Freestone there. He lived in Willington until he died in 1952.
Driver Frederick Charles Gammons 2369/522196	In the War, he served with the 483 Field Company Royal Engineers, going to France in July 1915 and was listed in the 1918 Willington Absent Voters' Register.
Driver Leslie George Gammons 522633 Brother of Frederick Charles Gammons	In the 1911 census, he is listed as a house boy domestic, living in Moggerhanger and single. In the War, he was with the Royal Engineers, enlisting in October 1915 and serving in England until he went to France in September 1918. Later that year he was hospitalised and discharged in April 1919 with nephritis, no longer fit for military service.

Rank, Name and Number	Comments
Lance Corporal Edward Golder Brother of William and Arthur M2/155928	In the 1911 census, he is listed as a tractor engine driver, living in Willington and was single. In the War, he was with the 27th Company Motor Transport ASC. He was discharged to the reserve in March 1917 to work as a steam ploughman for Mr N.J. Hull of Bedford, following an urgent request through the Board of Agriculture and Fisheries.
† Private William Golder 50142 Brother of Edward and Arthur	In the 1911 census, he is listed as a milk salesman, living in Willington and was married. In the War, he was with the 11th Battalion, Middlesex Regiment and was killed in action on April 9th, 1917 during the Arras offensive. He is buried at Sainte Catherine British Cemetery.
† Private Arthur Golder 25575/26564 Brother of William and Edward	In the 1911 census, he is listed as an agricultural labourer, living in Willington and single. In the War, he was first with the Northamptonshire Regiment and then with the 9th Battalion, Kings Own (Royal Lancashire Regiment) and was killed in action on April 28th, 1917 in Salonica. He is buried at Karasouli Military Cemetery, Greece.
Private Thomas Henry Golder* 8011 440478	He had served as a soldier in India before the War with the Oxfordshire and Buckinghamshire Light Infantry. He was vaccinated against typhoid in Willington at the end of 1911. He went to France in 1914 with the Oxfordshire and Buckinghamshire Light Infantry and got a gunshot wound in the thigh in November. After returning to his regiment, he suffered from nephritis and returned to England, where he was first posted to the 2/7th Battalion, Essex Regiment and then transferred to the Labour Corps in 1917, serving in an Agricultural Company for a time. He is only to be found on the 1918 Willington Absent Voters' Register, where he is listed as with the 2nd Company of London Yeomanry (126051), which does not tally with other military records. He is on neither Willington Roll of Honour.

Rank, Name and Number	Comments
Private Frank Henry Gudgin 118941	In the 1911 census, he is listed as a farm labourer, living in Willington and single and was subsequently a gamekeeper. He joined up in 1915 and saw service at home and in France. He got a shrapnel wound in the hand and from August 6th, 1918 to November 17th, 1918 was a prisoner of war in Germany, suffering cold and exposure. He was posted to the 2nd Battalion, Bedfordshire Regiment.
† Private Daniel Gudgin 202644 Brother of Frank Henry	In the 1911 census, he is listed as a nurseryman's labourer, living in Willington and single. He later became a railway porter. In the War, he was with the 9th Battalion, Essex Regiment and was killed in action on April 5th, 1918 during the German Spring offensive. He was buried at Ribemont Communal Cemetery Extension, Somme.
Private Albert Tom Hales 15931/45931	In the 1911 census, he is listed as an insurance agent, living in Willington and was married. In the War, he was first with the East Anglian Division Cyclists Company and then with the 1/7th Essex, serving in Egypt. He is listed on the 1918 Willington Absent Voters' Register.
Guardsman Percy Harding 25575	He served overseas with the Grenadier Guards and was discharged in December 1918, suffering with hernia. He is listed on the 1918 Willington Absent Voters' Register.
Sapper Arthur Sidney Harding (T)2484/522948	In the 1911 census, he is listed as a nursery work labourer, living in Moggerhanger and was married but was living in Willington, when he enlisted in 1915 and was tested as a painter. In the War he served with the 643rd (East Anglian) and 547th (Kent) Field Company, Royal Engineers and was hospitalised in 1918. On his discharge in 1919, he gave a Kempston address.
James Harding*	He is on the Willington 1914 electoral register and on the 1918 Absent Voters' Register, but no military details are given, and he is on neither Willington Roll of Honour.
Private Albert Eli Hart* 03493	He was born in Willington but lived in Bedford when he joined up in 1916 and served with the Army Veterinary Corps. He is not listed on either Willington Roll of Honour.

Rank, Name and Number	Comments
Gunner George William Hartwell 179894	In the 1911 census, he is listed as a nurseryman's labourer, living in Willington and was single. He served in France with the Y/42 Trench Mortar Battery, Royal Field Artillery (RFA). He appears to have been briefly hospitalised with an eye problem.
✝ Private Harry Hayden 17752	In the 1911 census, he is listed as a farm labourer, living in Eltisley and was single. He served with the 6th Battalion, Bedfordshire Regiment and died of wounds on August 21st, 1916 on the Western Front during the battle of the Somme. He is listed as Harry Edward Hayden on the CWGC database and is buried in the Boulogne Eastern Cemetery.
AC2 George Jakings 336278	He is on the Rolls of Honour and listed on the 1919 electoral roll as resident in Willington. He joined the RAF aged 17 in 1919 as an aircraft hand and had previously been a deck boy from November 1918.
Private George Jenkins *	According to the Parish Council minutes, he served on the "training ship Warspite". He is on neither Willington Roll of Honour.
Gunner Edward Linnett Lack 154139	In the 1911 census, he is listed as a nursery gardener, living in Kempston and single. He worked as Willington foreman for Isaac Godber and served as a Gunner with the Royal Garrison Artillery. After the War, he set up his own nursery business. He lost a son in World War II.
Private Cecil Thomas Little 168408	In the 1911 census, he is listed as at school, living in Willington and was single. He served with the Norfolk Regiment and the RAMC. He served on the Western Front and then with the Army of Occupation on the Rhine until he was demobilised in 1919.
Private George Martin 34160/73939	He served with the Bedfordshire militia from 1906 to 1908. In the 1911 census, he is listed as a farm labourer, living in Moggerhanger and was single. At the time of his attestation in 1915, he was married and living in Willington and is listed on the 1918 Willington Absent Voters' Register. He served with the Middlesex Regiment and with the Machine Gun Corps in France, being wounded in the arm in April 1918.

Rank, Name and Number	Comments
Rifleman Frank Martin 29462/200460	He served with the Bedfordshire militia from 1906 to 1908. In the 1911 census, he is listed as a farm labourer, living in Willington and was single then but had married and had children by the time of his attestation in 1915. He served with the Bedfordshire Regiment and then with the 10th, 5th and 13th Rifle Brigade (Prince Consort's Own), serving in France from 1916. He was invalided back to England suffering from trench feet at the end of 1916 and treated before re-joining.
Driver Arthur Mervyn Matthews 159062	In the 1911 census, he is listed as a farm labourer, living in Willington and was single. He served with the 126th Brigade, Royal Field Artillery.
Gunner Ernest Matthews 209953	In the 1911 census, he was a nursery gardener, living in Willington and married. He served with the 2nd Depot, Royal Garrison Artillery.
Private Henry Walter (Harry) Mayes 31538	In the 1911 census, he is listed as at school, living in Cople and was single. He served with the 7th Battalion, Bedfordshire Regiment.
Private Charles Herbert Norman G/25953	In the 1911 census, he was a farm labourer, living in Willington and was single. He served with the Bedfordshire Regiment and the 3rd Battery Buffs.
Private Walter Norman 31458/25370/56522	In the 1911 census, he is listed as at school, living in Willington and was single. He had become a nursery gardener by the time he signed up in 1916. He served with the Bedfordshire Regiment, the Duke of Wellington's 10th West Riding Regiment and the 8th York and Lancaster Regiment.

Rank, Name and Number	Comments
Company Quartermaster Sergeant (CQMS) Reginald Peacock* 778/522032	He came from Ravensden and was a farm labourer in the 1911 census. He joined the territorials in 1913 and served in the War with the Royal Engineers in France and Germany. He got a gunshot wound in the back in 1915 but returned to France and was mentioned in despatches and awarded the Military Medal for bravery. He gave his address as Manor Farm, Willington in 1919, where his wife, Louisa née Robinson lived. They had married in Willington on July 26th,1919; his residence in the marriage register is Clapham and hers is Willington. After his demobilisation, they lived in Bedford. He is not listed on either Willington Roll of Honour.
Private Charles Walter Purser 5678 Brother of Leonard	In the 1911 census, he may be listed as a carman, living in Lambeth and married. He served with the 11th (Prince Albert's Own) Hussars.
Private William Purser 483282	In the 1911 census, he is listed as a farm labourer, living in Willington and was married. He served with the Bedfordshire Regiment and the 432 Agricultural Labour Corps.
Private Albert Edward Purser 17160	In the 1911 census, he was a groom, living in Willington and single. He served with a Canadian Regiment, signing up with the Canadian Overseas Expeditionary Force in September 1914. He is listed on the 1918 Willington Absent Voters' Register.
† Private Leonard Arthur Purser 87066/37597 Brother of Charles Walter	Leonard served with the RAMC and the Rifle Brigade. He was killed in action in Palestine on May 2nd, 1918. He is listed on the Willington 1918 Absent Voters' Register but had also lived in Kempston. He was buried in the Jerusalem War Cemetery.
Driver George Quince T3/023916	In the 1911 census, he is listed as a house painter, living in Willington and was married. He served in France with the 151 Company ASC attached to 56th Field. Ambulance.

Rank, Name and Number	Comments
✝ Corporal Herbert Ray 14772/5539/202347	In the 1911 census, he is listed as a farm labourer, living in Gamlingay and single. He served with the Royal Garrison Artillery and in the 8th, 4th and 2nd Battalions, Suffolk Regiment. He was killed in action on June 15th, 1918 on the Western Front in the Pas de Calais. On the CWGC website and regimental medal roll he is listed as a corporal with the Suffolk Regiment.
Private Albert Robinson	He served with the Royal North Lancashire Regiment and is listed on both Rolls of Honour in Willington.
Driver Cecil Sharman 124254 - Brother of Charles and Joshua	In the 1911 census and at his attestation in December 1915, he is listed as a baker, living in Willington and was single. He served with the 65th Brigade, 466th Battery Royal Field Artillery.
Sergeant Charles Sharman 17781 - Brother of Cecil and Joshua	In the 1911 census, he is listed as a market garden labourer, living in Willington and was single. He served with the 1st Battalion, Bedfordshire Regiment, was wounded in September 1916 and is listed as a corporal on the 1918 Willington Absent Voters' Register.
Driver Joshua Joseph Sharman 3427/528505 - Brother of Cecil and Charles	In the 1911 census, he was a market garden labourer, living in Willington and single. He served with the 11th Company, Royal Engineers Signals and is listed on the 1918 Willington Absent Voters' Register and on his regimental medal roll as driver. He died aged 48 in 1939, having lived in Willington and worked on the land for most of his life.
Private Fred Simmons 480737	In the 1911 census, he was a Willington farm labourer and married. He served with the Royal Defence Corps and 482 Labour Corps and lived near Castle Mills according to the 1918 Absent Voters' Register for that area.
Private Arthur Edward Spavins 33185 - Brother of Frank and Harry	In the 1911 census, he is listed as a farm labourer, living in Willington and was single. He served with the 2/4th and 8th Battalion, Leicestershire Regiment and is listed on the 1918 Willington Absent Voters' Register and regimental medal roll as private. He was awarded the Silver War Badge and discharged because of wounds received in December 1917.

Rank, Name and Number	Comments
Private Frank Barringer Spavins 59846/17126 - Brother of Arthur and Harry	Frank served with the Bedfordshire militia from 1906 to 1908. In the 1911 census, he is listed as a farm labourer, living in Willington and was single. He served with the Royal Fusiliers and Labour Corps. He suffered from trench feet and lost his toes.
Sapper Harry Sidney Spavins 75816 - Brother of Frank and Arthur	In the 1911 census, he is listed as a farm labourer, living in Willington and was single. He served with the Royal Engineers 47 Division Signal Service. Because of his previous experience as a telegraphist at his mother's Post Office, he took part in hot air balloon reconnaissance, signalling details of enemy positions. He is listed on the 1918 Willington Absent Voters' Register and listed there and on his regimental medal roll as 'Spr' (sapper).
Private William Frederick Spavins - aka Billy Day – cousin of the Spavins brothers and brother-in-law of Charles Wooding 339093	In the 1911 census, he is listed as a farm labourer, living in Willington and was single. He served with the Bedfordshire Regiment and the 586 Employment Company Labour Corps.
✝ Private Frederick Herbert Stokes 3054 G/30249	In the 1911 census, he is listed as at school, living in Willington and single. He served with the Yeoman Cyclists and 7th Battalion, Queen's Own Royal West Kent Battalion and was killed in action on March 28th, 1918 in the Oise area during the German Spring offensive. He was listed on the 1918 Willington Absent Voters' Register. He is commemorated on the Pozières Memorial.
Gunner Percy Alfred Summerfield* 171395	He was born in Willington and served with the Royal Garrison Artillery in France. By the time, he attested in December 1915, he had moved to Wales and worked in a colliery. He caught trench fever during the War. He is not listed on any Willington memorials.

Rank, Name and Number	Comments
Driver Alfred Swannell 2368/522570 Brother of Edgar	In the 1911 census, he is listed as a farm labourer, living in Willington and was single. He served with the Royal Engineers in the 488 East Anglian Field Company.
✝ Private Edgar Swannell 17747 Brother of Alfred	In the 1911 census, he is listed as a farm labourer, living in Willington and was single. He served with the 1st Battalion, Bedfordshire Regiment, and was killed in action on May 12th 1918 on the Western Front during the German Spring offensive. He is buried at Merville Communal Cemetery Extension.
Horace Swannell*	He is only to be found on 1918 Willington Absent Voters' Register.
Private George William Usher 456990	In the 1911 census, he was living in Willington and was single. He served with the Bedfordshire Regiment and with the 693 Agricultural Labour Corps.
Sergeant Arthur Usher 5493/33199	In the 1911 census, he is listed as a market garden labourer, living in Willington and married. His records indicate he worked for Mark Young. He joined the 5th Battalion, Bedfordshire Regiment in 1915 and later transferred to the 3rd Battalion, Leicestershire Regiment, transferring to other Leicestershire Battalions later. He served as an infantryman in France and in 1917, got a shrapnel wound in his leg and in 1918, a gunshot wound to his hand. He lived in Carlton at the time of the 1918 Absent Voters' Register for that area.
Private John Webb 25880	In the 1911 census, he is listed as a market garden labourer, living in Cople and was single. He served with the Bedfordshire Regiment and was wounded in May 1917.
✝ Private Robert Webb 5546/27601	In the 1911 census, he is listed as a nurseryman's labourer, living in Willington and was single. He served with the 1/6th Battalion, South Staffordshire Regiment and the 1st Battalion, Royal Warwickshire Regiment and was killed in action on October 23rd, 1916 on the Western Front. He fought at Ypres and on the Somme and is commemorated on the Thiepval Memorial.

Rank, Name and Number	Comments
† Private Walter William Weedon S8011 M/324896	He was born in Kingston-on-Thames and in the 1911 census was a nurseryman, living in Norwood and single. He served in France with the 1st Battalion, Rifle Brigade and later, after being ill, with the 9 GHQ. MT ASC, where he drove heavy lorries. He was discharged from the ASC on May 7th, 1919 as no longer fit for military service. The Medical Board described him as in poor general condition with valvular disease of the heart (VDH) and oedema to the legs and said his condition was attributable to military service. He had previously suffered from myalgia and bronchitis. He died from heart disease at the Gables, Willington, the home of his sister and brother-in-law, on May 26th, 1919, aged 38. He is not on the CWGC database.
Private Charles Wooding 18210 Brother-in-law of William Frederick Spavins	In the 1911 census, he is listed as a cowman on a farm, living in Willington and single but married later that year. He served in France from September 1914 with the 2nd Battalion, Bedfordshire Regiment. He was wounded at the battle of Loos in September 1915 and was also gassed. He was moved to hospital in Lincoln. He was discharged because of his wound in September 1916. After the War, he ran a market gardening business from Croots Farm and died in 1970.

Endnotes

[1] The first section makes use of material I previously included in Bollington. R. (2012) *Willington and the Russells,* Willington: Gostwick Press.

[2] The Record, July 28th, 1914.

[3] Biggleswade Chronicle, October 2nd, 1914.

[4] Unless otherwise indicated, the phrase "Bedford newspaper" used throughout this publication refers to the Bedfordshire Times and Independent.

[5] Bedfordshire Times and Independent, March 19th, 1915.

[6] Bedfordshire Archives Service: WW1/RH1/100.

[7] Appendix 1 shows the church Roll of Honour. Appendix 2 provides some additional names by also using Parish Council records, the 1918 Absent Voters' Register and information from military records, bringing the potential total of men who served to seventy-eight.

[8] See the Bedfordshire Times and Independent of July 14th and 21st,1922 for details of Eleanor Paine's life and work.

[9] Bessie Godber was the wife of Isaac Godber. Their family moved into the manor house in Willington before the war.

[10] Bedfordshire Times and Independent, August 7th, 1914, reprinted from the Times.

[11] After the emergency instructions were modified in 1916, one task became organising gangs of workers rather than dealing with food stuff.

[12] Bedfordshire Archives Service: WW1/AC/OP2/26.

[13] The Queen's Engineering Works Magazine. No 5. January 1918. Bedfordshire Archives Service: Z791/12.

[14] Bedfordshire Times and Independent, May 14th, 1915.

[15] Presumably Joyce's brothers.

[16] The seven were Alonzo Ball, Fred Cooper, Thomas Henry Golder, William Purser, Fred Simmons, William Frederick Spavins and George William Usher. All but one had been in another regiment first, which probably indicates that they were wounded and moved into the Labour Corps as a result.

[17] Biggleswade Chronicle, March 3rd, 1916.

[18] Bedfordshire Times, June 16th, 1916.

[19] Report on Women's Labour made for Col Fenwick for purposes of recruiting. December 1916. Bedfordshire Archives Service: WW1/WA/2/1

[20] Certificate of National Service in the Women's Land Army. Bedfordshire Archives Service: WW1/WA4/1/8.

[21] Record of Women's Efficiency Tests conducted on behalf of the Bedfordshire Women's War Agricultural Committee. May 1918. Bedfordshire Archives Service: WW1/WA/3/1.

[22] http://www.womenslandarmy.co.uk/world-war-one/ - accessed December 5th, 2017

[23] Bedfordshire Times, January 11th, 1918.

[24] Biggleswade Chronicle, June 28th, 1918.

[25] Ibid.

[26] *Great War Diaries: 2nd Bn, Grenadier Guards War Diary 1914-1919* (pp11/12). Great War Diaries Ltd: Kindle Edition.

[27] See http://www.bedfordregiment.org.uk/1stbn/1stbattalion.html, accessed on December 26th, 2017, for further details

[28] Biggleswade Chronicle, January 29th, 1915. The captain referred to was Captain Basil John Orlebar.

[29] The other, Reginald Peacock, served in the Royal Engineers in France and Germany and was mentioned in despatches and awarded the Military Medal. His connection to the village is through his wife, who was living at Manor Farm in 1919. He was not named on any of the village memorials and moved to Bedford after the war.

[30] Extract from the 1st Battalion, Bedfordshire Regiment War Diary. Bedfordshire Archives Service: X550/2/5.

[31] See https://www.forces-war-records.co.uk/units/1615/middlesex-regiment/, accessed December 26th, 2017.

[32] See https://www.forces-war-records.co.uk/blog/2015/04/09/on-this-day-1917-first-battle-of-the-scarpe-the-successful-beginning-of-the-arras-offensive, accessed December 26th, 2017.

[33] Those recorded as in the ASC were Frederick Barcock, Victor Cross, James Freeston and Edward Golder. Walter Weedon moved there from the Rifle Brigade.

[34] See https://en.wikipedia.org/wiki/Battle_of_Doiran_(1917), accessed December 26th, 2017.

[35] See https://www.cwgc.org/find-a-cemetery/cemetery/68800/karasouli-military-cemetery/, accessed January 8th, 2018.

[36] The men known to have been in the Agricultural Labour Corps at one time were Alonzo Ball, Fred Cooper, Thomas Henry Golder, William Purser and George William Usher.

[37] See appendices 1 and 2 for further details of the men who served.

[38] The overall figures given here are taken from Sheffield, G. (2014) *A Short History of the First World War*, London: One World Publications. p.129.

[39] Order of service for the 1920 memorial service at St Lawrence, Willington. Bedfordshire Archives Service: Z153/46.

[40] The words are from 1 Samuel 25:16 and were often used on war memorials.

[41] Extract from the memories of Reginald Lymon, the nephew of Frank Barringer Spavins.

[42] Biggleswade Chronicle, April 7th, 1922.

[43] Those listed are found on one or more of the Rolls of Honour and memorials in the church and Peace Memorial Hall, the 1918 Absent Voters' Register, the minute book of the Parish Council and surviving military records. Information has also been added relating to those who died by using the CWGC database. There are some differences in the sources. The fallen are shown with the following before their name: ✝. Where differences relating to rank have been found, the rank given in medal records has been used if available. Those marked * appear on neither village Roll of Honour but appear to have had some type of connection with Willington.

The photograph on the back cover is of Sapper Harry Sidney Spavins of the Royal Engineers, who is named on the Willington Rolls of Honour.